Kintsukuroi Christians

TURNING MENTAL BROKENNESS INTO BEAUTY

Dr C. Edward Pitt

Ark House Press
PO Box 1722, Port Orchard, WA 98366 USA
PO Box 1321, Mona Vale NSW 1660 Australia
PO Box 318 334, West Harbour, Auckland 0661 New Zealand
arkhousepress.com

Please note: The information contained in this book is general in nature. It does not constitute individual medical advice. Any information contained in this book should be discussed with the reader's treating physician before implementation as part of the reader's individual medical care, and any use of the information contained in this book is at the user's discretion. Information regarding crisis services are accurate at the time of publication. The author/publisher specifically disclaim any and all liability that may arise either directly or indirectly from the use of, or application of information from, or the interpretation of information from, this work.

Cataloguing in Publication Data:
Title: Kintsukuroi Christians
ISBN: 9780994596895 (pbk.)
Subjects: Christian Living, Mental Illness, Healing
Other Authors/Contributors: Pitt, Dr C. Edward

Design by initiateagency.com

Contents

Kintsukuroi Christians

When I was a kid growing up, there wasn't much that my father couldn't repair.

Dad was extremely gifted with his hands, a talent that I certainly didn't inherit. He was able to take a problem, come up with a practical solution in his mind's eye, then build it out of whatever scraps of wood, metal or plastic he could lay his hands on. It was the ultimate expression of frugality and recycling that comes from a limited income and four growing children.

Dad could do some amazing things. One time he turned our side lawn into a courtyard by recycling whatever he could source. He made a wooden lattice fence from old wooden pallets, and he made his own pavers from a bit of cement and some gravel he borrowed from the local creek bed behind our house. He then laid the pavers himself in a perfect mosaic pattern like he'd been doing it all his life.

Another time when he took up bee keeping to help sustain his honey addiction, he built his own solar-powered wax-recycling contraption out of some old wooden crates, tin sheeting, black paint and a pane of glass. He built his own centrifugal honey extractor from an industrial sized plastic bucket and some old bicycle parts.

Unfortunately, I don't have space for the thousand or so other things that he built over the years, but they were all ingenious, and spurred on by the desire to enjoy life. He was always coming up with new ideas and creative solutions to interesting challenges.

Dad was also able to resurrect nearly everything that broke in our house. Plates, cups, teapots, toys, tools … it seemed there wasn't anything that couldn't be fixed by the careful application of Araldite.

Araldite, for those unfamiliar with it, is some sort of epoxy resin that, in the right hands, possesses mystical properties of adhesion. It would stick anything to anything.

Dad's gift for repairing things with Araldite meant that a lot of our things were patched up. Some of our most loved possessions were the most cracked. Despite being glued together several times, each item was still functional. Maybe not as pretty as it may have once been, but still useful, and more importantly, still treasured. Each time the Araldite came out, it taught me that whilst all things have the capacity to be broken, they also have the capacity for redemption.

Kintsukuroi

There's an ancient Japanese tradition that shares the same principles. For more than 400 years, the Japanese people have practiced *kintsukuroi*. Kintsukuroi *(pronounced 'kint soo koo ree')* is the art of repairing broken pottery with gold or silver lacquer, and the deep understanding that the piece is more beautiful for having been broken.

The edges of the broken fragments are coated with the glue made from Japanese lacquer resin and are bonded back into place. The joints are rubbed with an adhesive until the surface is perfectly smooth again.

After drying, more lacquer is applied. This process is repeated many times, and gold dust is also applied.

In kintsukuroi, the gold lacquer accentuates the fracture lines, and the breakage is honoured as part of that piece's history.

I'm a medical doctor, working in a busy family practice on the outskirts of Brisbane, Australia. One afternoon, a young woman came into my office. She was a young, professional woman in her late 20's, of Pakistani descent, who was a new patient to my practice. It was late in the day, you know, that time when the caffeine level has hit a critical low and the only way you can concentrate on the rest of the day is the knowledge you'll be going home soon.

She wasn't keen to discuss her problems, but she didn't know what else to do. As she slowly opened up and shared her story, she revealed a glimpse into the inner torment that she'd been suffering. For months, she had been experiencing anxiety and fear but without a clear reason.

She couldn't eat. She couldn't sleep. Her heart raced all the time. She was afraid of nearly everything, including doctors, psychologists, and especially medications. After talking with her for a few minutes, it was fairly obvious that she was suffering from Generalised Anxiety Disorder, and I mean, she was literally suffering.

I was quite concerned for her. She allowed me to do some basic tests to rule out any physical cause that may have been contributing to her symptoms, but that's as far as she would let me help her. Despite talking at length about her diagnosis, she could not accept the fact that she had a psychiatric condition, and would not accept any treatment for it. She chose not to follow up with me either. I only saw her twice.

To this day, I'm unsure what it was that prevented the acceptance of her diagnosis. Perhaps it was fear for her job, social isolation, or a cultural factor. Perhaps it was the anxiety itself. Whatever the reason, despite having severe ongoing symptoms, she could not come to terms with the fact that she was mentally ill.

She was a victim twice over, suffering because of the mental illness, and its stigma.

Mental illness is a mystery to most people, shrouded by mythology, stigma, gossip or Hollywood hype. It's all around us, affecting a quarter of the population every year, but so often those with mental illness hide in plain sight. Mental illness doesn't give you a limp, a lump, or a lag. It affects feelings and thoughts, our most latent personal inner world, the iceberg underneath the waters.

On the front line of medicine, I see people with mental health problems every day, but mental health problems don't limit themselves to the doctor's office. They're spread throughout our everyday lives. If one in four people have a mental health problem of one form or another, then one in four Christians have a mental health problem of one form or another. If your church experience is anything like mine, you would shake hands with at least ten people from the front door to your seat. Statistically speaking, two or three of them will have a mental illness. Could you tell?

It's a fair bet that most people wouldn't know if someone in their church had a mental illness. Christians battling with mental illness learn to present a happy façade, (or face the judgment if they don't), so they either hide their inner pain, or just avoid church altogether.

Experiencing a mental illness also makes people feel permanently broken. They feel like they're never going to be whole again, or good enough, or useful, or loved. They're often treated that way by well-meaning but ill-informed church members whose idea's and opinions on mental illness is out-of-date.

The truth is that Christians who have experienced mental ill-health are like a kintsukuroi pot.

Mental illness may break them, sure. But they don't stay broken. The dark and difficult times, and their recovery from their illness is simply God putting lacquer on their broken pieces, putting them back together, and rubbing gold dust into their cracks.

We are all kintsukuroi Christians — we're more beautiful and more honoured than we were before, *because* of our brokenness, and our recovery.

My story

Mental illness is a dark, lonely and tormenting place. I know, because I've suffered from it. I went through debilitating anxiety during my adolescence, and deep depression as an adult.

In my mid-to-late thirties, I suffered from depression for about four years. In the two years I was at my lowest, I was moody and emotional. I exploded in anger or melted in tears. I was sullen. I hardly ever laughed, because I didn't find anything funny. It felt like my soul had been drained from me.

I couldn't face anyone socially. I am not a socialite at the best of times, but the thought of having to go out to engage with friends and family was draining, sometimes physically distressing. When I was dragged out, I was withdrawn.

This is where the stigma of depression and depression itself feed into each other. I was so depressed that I didn't want to interact with people, and when I did, I was sullen and withdrawn. This wasn't interpreted as depression by other people, but as arrogance. Besides, even if they knew I was depressed, it's not exactly an endearing quality. Who would want to hang around with someone who had the charm and charisma of a dead fish?

The complete absence of joy and pleasure in anything was difficult enough. But the existential angst was even more tormenting. I questioned my salvation. I questioned God's love. I was plagued by the fear that I would die a lonely useless failure, unloved and unlovable. I occasionally questioned the existence of God himself.

I knew what the Bible said, and if anything, that haunted me more. I couldn't understand why I could love God, serve Him and live for Him, and still not have any joy. God is perfect, so the obvious conclusion was that it was my fault that I was feeling this way. It must have been my sin, my selfishness, my … something! The self-loathing that resulted from this way of thinking compounded my already poor mood and made me feel even worse than I already was.

Ironically, all of this was aggravated by church. Incessantly chirpy people with permanent beaming smiles were everywhere. In a typical large church, you can be peppered by the standard church greeting up to twenty times before you even reach your seat. It always follows the same pattern: "Hey! How are you today? Isn't it a great day to be in church? / Isn't God good? / Isn't it wonderful to be alive?"

Despite being rhetorical questions, they still reminded me just how awful I felt. I toyed with the idea of replying truthfully, "Oh, I'm just having an existential crisis". Though I knew that if I did, I'd have ended up explaining myself to some well meaning but ill-equipped wannabe counsellor, or being assessed as a dysfunctional twerp. So I just kept suppressing my pain and lied, "Oh, I'm just a bit tired … you know … work …".

Thoughts of "It would be so much easier if I wasn't here" came to me at different times. I never seriously contemplated suicide, but I understand why people do. Depression deprives you of hope. I was literally hopeless. Paul wrote that there abides three things—faith, hope and love. I had none of them.

During all of this time I kept working. I didn't go to work because I gained any satisfaction from it. I went more out of mindless habit. I could smile for patients, carry on a pithy conversation, and even counsel people about their own depression, all the while hiding my own.

The first meaningful step in my recovery came when I went to see a psychologist. I don't remember what we talked about specifically, although I do remember going through most of the tissues he had in his office as I unloaded years of emotional turmoil and despair with someone who accepted me without judgment or disdain.

I also came to understand "the wilderness". I was depressed, but I was in good company. Moses, David and Elijah spent time in the physical wilderness, and each of them went through periods of mental destitution as well as physical deprivation. But I identify with Peter most of all.

Peter was with Jesus, the Messiah himself, every day for nearly three years. He heard all of Jesus' words, he saw the miracles and even witnessed the transfiguration of Jesus where the physical and spiritual realms blended together in magnificent glory. He must have felt the surge of the Holy Spirit's power as he watched Jesus teach, heal, and love the people that swarmed him. Such a privileged place in history must have made the pain of his crash all the more intense. Peter must have experienced some of the deepest loss, most abject sense of failure and most profound alienation that any human could feel when he rejected the Messiah, his friend. Even seeing the empty tomb on Resurrection Sunday couldn't overcome his sense of despair and worthlessness. He drifted back to his old life of fishing, giving up on life with God completely.

I found hope in Peter's restoration. Jesus went to Peter and found him desolate and frustrated, toiling all night with absolutely nothing to show for it. Jesus not only gave Peter the biggest catch of fish in his life, but showed him such a profound depth of understanding and kindness over breakfast on the shore. Peter may have abandoned Jesus, but Jesus never abandoned Peter. If Jesus still loved Peter in spite of all his flaws, then surely Jesus still loved me.

A new hope

I've come out the other side of my depression now, with a much deeper, fuller appreciation of what it is to be human. The textbook description of depression I was familiar with was nothing compared with actually experiencing it. When I talk to people with depression now, I can wholeheartedly empathize.

When Rick Warren returned to the pulpit after the suicide of his son Matthew in 2012, he told his church that he would work to decrease the stigma of mental illness in the church. Having experienced the depths of depression myself, I share Rick Warren's desire. The church is the body of Christ, His hands and His feet, a place where the lost and the broken can come and find wholeness, healing and purpose.

In Isaiah 61, the prophet wrote about the task of the coming Messiah: "The Spirit of the Lord God is upon me; because the Lord hath anointed me to preach good tidings unto the meek; he hath sent me to bind up the broken hearted, to proclaim liberty to the captives, and the opening of the prison to them that are bound ... to comfort all that mourn; To appoint unto them that mourn in Zion, to give them beauty for ashes, the oil of joy for mourning, the garment of praise for the spirit of heaviness; that they might be called trees of righteousness, the planting of the Lord, that he might be glorified." (Isaiah 61:1-3)

When Jesus was on the earth, He did just that. He healed all who came to Him, He freed people from tormenting spirits and he supernaturally fed thousands of people. When Peter went to the house of Cornelius in Acts 10, he summarised the ministry of Jesus by saying, "how God anointed Jesus of Nazareth with the Holy Ghost and with power: who went about doing good, and healing all that were oppressed of the devil; for God was with him." (Acts 10:38)

Jesus told his disciples that, "Most assuredly, I say to you, he who believes in Me, the works that I do he will do also; and greater works than these he will do, because I go to My Father." (John 14:12)

So, our job as Christians is to preach hope and healing, to proclaim freedom to those who are oppressed, and to give them beauty, joy and praise in place of shame and brokenness, and in **greater** measure than Jesus ever did. Mental illness binds, breaks, imprisons and oppresses more than its fair share of us. If there was ever a final untouched people group, it's those who hide in plain sight, oppressed and imprisoned in their own minds. It's the mission field of the depressed and anxious.

Recovery Road

I've written this book to try and bring together the best of the medical and spiritual.

Unfortunately, good scientific information often bypasses the church. The church is typically misled by Christian 'experts' that preach a view of mental health based on a skewed or outdated understanding of mental illness and cognitive neuroscience. I want to present a guide to mental illness and recovery that's easy for Christians to digest, adopting the best spiritual AND scientific perspective.

In this book, I'll be looking at some scientific basics. Our mental world is based on the physical world. Our mind is a function of the brain, just like breathing is a function of our lungs. Just as we can't properly understand our breathing without understanding our lungs, so it is that if we're going to understand our thinking and our minds, we are going to have to understand the way our brain works. So the first part of this book will be an unpacking of the neurobiology of thought.

We'll also look at what promotes good mental health. Then we'll look at what causes mental illness, specifically looking at the most common mental health disorders. I will only look at some of the most common disorders to demonstrate some general principles of psychiatric illnesses and treatments. This book won't be an encyclopaedia, and it doesn't need to be. I hope to provide a framework so that common and uncommon mental health disorders can be better understood.

I also discuss suicide, which is sadly more common than most people realise, and is rarely discussed.

Mental illness can be challenging. Sometimes learning about mental illness can bring up difficult feelings or emotions, either things that you've been through yourself, or because you develop a better understanding of what a loved one is going through or has been through. Sometimes old issues that have been suppressed or not properly dealt with can bubble up to the surface. If at any point you feel distressed, I strongly encourage you to talk to your local doctor, psychologist, or pastor. If the feelings are so overwhelming that you need to talk to someone quickly, then please don't delay, but reach out to a crisis service in your country.

In Australia

- you can call either Lifeline on 13 11 14, or
- BeyondBlue provides a number of different support options

o the BeyondBlue Support Service provides advice and support via telephone 24/7 (call 1300 22 4636)

o daily web chat (between 3pm–12am) and

o email (with a response provided within 24 hours) via their website https://www.beyondblue.org.au/about-us/contact-us.

In the US

• call the National Suicide Prevention Lifeline by calling 1-800-273-TALK (8255).

In New Zealand

• call Lifeline Aotearoa 24/7 Helpline on 0800 543 354

In the UK

• Samaritans offer a 24 hour help line, on 116 123

For other countries, *Your Life Counts* maintains a list of crisis services across a number of countries: http://www.yourlifecounts.org/need-help/crisis-lines.

I know mental illness is difficult, and we often look at ourselves or others as though the brokenness is abhorrent, ugly and deforming.

My hope is that by the end of this book, you'll see the broken pieces are mended with gold, and realise that having or recovering from a mental illness doesn't render someone useless or broken, but that God turns our mental brokenness into beauty.

2

Brain Biology 101

There is something special about music. It's a language without words, speaking directly to our souls. A violin in the hands of a virtuoso can be emotionally transcendent. The violin in the hands of a seven-year old beginner can make your skin crawl and your soul cringe. Good or bad, music can move you.

Here's a question: is it the instrument that makes the music, or does the music make the instrument? A violin can make some beautiful music. Can that music make a violin, or exist independently of the violin?

That's not meant to be some deep philosophical question. It's pretty simple, isn't it? The violin produces the music. Without the violin, there would be no music. In this small scenario, the music can't exist without a fully functional violin.

In the same way, our mind and our thoughts are dependent on our brain. Without a functioning brain, we don't have any thoughts or any function of the mind. Our mind does not control our brain, but instead, the mind is dependent on the brain.

It seems a very simple concept to grasp, however it's an important principle to understand early on in our journey because understanding mental function, health and illness rests on it. There are some well-known Christian preachers who teach that the mind controls the brain and is independent of the brain. Unfortunately, this teaching is scientifically back-to-front–like saying that our speech controls our mouth or our breath controls our lungs. Don't be misled. We have to start from the correct mindset.

The first rule of mental health is that our mind, our thoughts, our feelings and our actions all stem from our physical brain.

This chapter will help us to get on the same level of understanding about how our brain works so that we can understand a bit more about our feelings, thoughts and actions. I could go on and on, waxing lyrical about the amazing science of the brain, but I promise I'll stick to the essentials and try to keep it light.

Forty watts

Despite our brain being one of the most sophisticated computers on the planet, it tends to run on relatively little power. Scientists estimate that the average brain runs on the same amount of power as a 40-watt light bulb.[1] "Why so low?" you might ask. It has to do with the amount of energy that our bodies can spare. There's only so much food we can eat to fuel ourselves, and that energy has to power the rest of our bodies as well as our brains. To compensate, God gave our brains the ability to automate. Once a skill has been learned or a memory formed, the brain can do the same tasks over and over again, easily and efficiently. Energy sapping attention is only used to process new or changing information.

We demonstrate this to ourselves everyday, although we barely notice. Are you aware of every step when you walk to your kitchen? Are you aware of your arm picking up your cup of coffee to lift it to your mouth, or your facial and oral muscles sipping and swallowing your full-flavoured brew? The usual answer is no (though if you're heading to the kitchen soon, you may notice it now that I've brought in to your attention).

The brain does this with even the most complex of tasks – like driving. I find this happens to me when I'm driving home from work. Going the same route every day means that I often drift into autopilot as I'm thinking about the events of the day or my stomach reminds me that I'm hungry, and five minutes later I pay attention to my surroundings and realise that I'm nearly home.

Most of what we do everyday is pretty much the same. We're really only consciously aware of a very small fraction of the work our brain does. Our brain does most of it's work at the 'subconscious' level, without conscious awareness or control. This includes making most of our decisions, and planning the actions we need to take (I'll discuss this in more detail later in the chapter).

Thinking about thinking

Have you ever stopped to ponder about what goes on inside our minds?

Like, if our brain is running on autopilot most of the time, then why do we have that voice in our heads when we think? Why does that One Direction song keep getting stuck in my brain? What drove me to listen to One Direction in the first place? Why are my thoughts mostly images and sounds but I can't 'touch' or 'taste' them?

We don't really notice them until someone points them out, but pictures and words come into and out of our heads continuously, sometimes like a babbling brook, sometimes like a river in full flood. In 1890, pioneering psychologist and philosopher William James was the first to describe our consciousness as a 'stream.'[2]

A 'stream' is a good analogy, because our consciousness continues to bubble away incessantly. We can divert our attention to something, but when the brain has nothing to focus on, our mind still has plenty to say. What makes our consciousness the way it is?

Components of consciousness

Philosophers have been pondering consciousness for thousands of years, but it's only in the last few decades that scientists have begun to understand how conscious awareness works.

The modern understanding of our stream of conscious thoughts goes back to the work of a British scientist called Alan Baddeley. Before the work of Baddeley, short term memory was known to exist but was not well understood. It was assumed that short term memory was just a simple reservoir for holding information until needed. Baddeley and his colleague Graham Hitch came up with a better model of short term memory back in 1974.

Baddeley recognised that when information is being held in short term memory, it's made up of different types of information, and that information could be manipulated, rather than just passively held. He coined the term 'Working Memory' to reflect that vital difference – the information wasn't just stored, but could be worked with, like a mental blackboard.

Baddeley thought of working memory as made up of a number of sub-systems which he referred to as 'slave systems', one for visual information, one for auditory information, and a third which could be used as an overflow buffer for more complex information. These sub-systems would be controlled by another unit, responsible for doing the hard work of manipulating the information in the sub-systems, deciding what information to put into the sub-systems, and what information would then go to other parts of the brain, including long term memory.

Think about your thoughts for a moment. What form do they take? Usually words or pictures, right? That's our inner monologue, and our 'mind's eye'. The inner monologue and the mind's eye corresponds to the sub-systems of working memory. When you "see" an image with your mind's eye, that's the visuospatial sketchpad. When you listen to your inner monologue, that's your phonological loop. When a song gets stuck in your head, that's your phonological loop as well, but on repeat mode.

When there's a lot of complex information needed to be stored in working memory (like remembering a long sentence), or some extra processing is required, the episodic buffer is engaged. The central executive is doing all of the organising, manipulating and arranging in the background.[3]

In 1982, an American researcher called Bernard J. Baars[4, 5] took the concept of working memory a step further by proposing the Global Workspace theory. Baars thought that our conscious stream of thought was a conscious broadcast of information from working memory which then engages a wider area of the cerebral cortex necessary to most efficiently process the information.

According to Baars, deep thinking is a projection from one of your brain's executive systems to the central executive of working memory, which then recalls the relevant information from long-term memory and directs the information through the various parts of the sub-systems of working memory to process the complex details involved.

For example, visualizing a complex scene of a mountain stream in your mind would involve the executive brain directing the central executive of working memory to recall information about mountains and streams and associated details, and project them into the visuospatial sketchpad and phonological loop. The central executive binds the two streams, and could also manipulate the scene if required to create plans, or think about the scene in new or unexpected ways (like imagining an elephant riding a bicycle along the riverbank).

Even though the scene appears as one continuous episode, it's actually broken up into multiple cognitive cycles, in the same way that images in a movie appear to be moving, but are really just multiple still frames played in sequence.

So our thought life, our stream of conscious awareness, is a projection of information coming from other parts of the brain, being utilised by working memory and the various sub-systems within it.

Baddley's Model of Working Memory

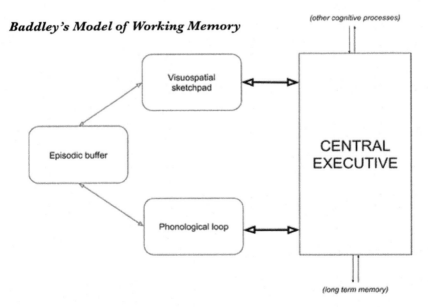

What makes our consciousness conscious?

Researchers have helped us understand the components of our conscious awareness, but the research doesn't tell us *why it's conscious, which is the hottest question in cognitive neuroscience today.*

It's beyond the scope of this book to try to explain why we experience the phenomenon of consciousness, and it's not relevant to our understanding of mental health either. But suffice to say, we know that our stream of thought is a function of the brain, and that our brain can processes vast amounts of information without us necessarily being consciously aware of it. For example, using a general anaesthetic drug, researchers have shown a direct correlation between the activity of a brain network involved in working memory and attention and the level of consciousness.[6]

Other research has shown that subjects who have been temporarily blinded by stunning the visual part of the brain could still detect whether a face shown on a screen in front of them was happy or sad and even where it was on a grid.[7, 8] So if the brain can process things without our conscious awareness, why do we need to be conscious?

I'm not sure if I have a philosophical or theological answer to that, but biologically, our brain is wired this way to give us the flexibility to solve new or complex problems. As I discussed earlier, our brain would rather do things on automatic pilot because that saves a lot of energy, but life is full of unexpected surprises, things that we haven't seen before that haven't been learnt, that can't be run from an automated script. Attention and working memory give us the ability to perform more complex processing of new or important information.[6]

"Thinking" and "Choosing"

There are many other aspects of the function of the brain that I would love to discuss more, but I'll leave that for another time.

There's just one last thing about how our brains work that will be important in coming chapters, and that's the concept of choice.

As humans, we have a strong feeling of voluntary control over our actions, that everything we do is something that we choose to do. This sense of control is so fundamental to our existence that much of our social system depends on it, such as our laws and the penalties for breaking them.[9]

Except that science has proven that our sense of full control is largely an illusion.

The illusion of full control

I understand this idea might be hard for some people to accept. We're taught that we have full control over our actions or ideas. We experience this sense of control from the vantage point of our own perception. It's hard to believe that we're not really in full control of our actions and choices.

For the purposes of this book, what's most important to understand about our choices is how much control we actually have over them. The dominant paradigm in the Christian church is the idea of free will. We're taught that the words we say and things we do are the exclusive product of our will. Cognitive neuroscience paints a different picture.

The modern neuroscience of the will started with Benjamin Libet. Professor Libet was a researcher in physiology at the University of California San Francisco. He was initially studying the electrical properties of different sensations in the brain, but in the early 1980's, he performed an experiment to look at the electrical readings that take place when a person decides on an action. His subjects would decide to perform a simple movement of their arm or hand, and say when they were aware of the intention to act. Electrodes connected to the subject's heads measured their brain activity before, during, and after their decision to act.

What was remarkable was that there was a clear spike in electrical activity occurring up to a full second before a test subject was consciously aware of the intention to act.[10] Libet suggested that an unconscious process was responsible for the 'willed' action.

Other studies since that time have confirmed Libet's results. In fact, a study in 2008 showed that predictable brain activity occurred up to eight seconds before a person was aware of their intention to act.[11]

This predictable unconscious spike of brain activity prior to awareness of our intention to act has been verified over and over and is beyond doubt, but there's still lots of debate as to exactly what it means. Defenders of the idea of free will have tried presenting alternative explanations of the pre-awareness unconscious activity, though most leading neuroscientists in the field disagree.

The neuroscience of action

So if we don't have full conscious control of our actions, what *does* go on in our brains when we perform an action?

Again, I won't go into the fine print, but it's important to understand that our brain does most of its work at a subconscious level, which includes the planning and execution of our actions.[12, 13] The brain takes the information presented to it, as well as information from memories, and makes a prediction of the best course of action. This means that our processing of goals, rewards, and actions can be affected by 'subliminal priming' (in other words, information we process below our conscious level can affect the decision about the best course of action).[13]

Even though we're not aware of every process the brain employs in our subconscious to formulate the best plan of action and to prime our system ready for that action, there is a element of awareness that provides real-time monitoring and a veto function.[12] Like if you were about to complain about your job and then suddenly remembered you were talking to your boss, you could stop yourself from saying something you might later regret.

What does it all mean?

The take-away message here is this:

We have limited will, not free will.

We still have some capacity to choose, but our conscious choices are dependent on our subconscious brain activity, our experience and knowledge.

We can make choices, or "exercise our will", if you like, but within the constraints of a number of factors beyond our conscious control. We can "pull the brake", so to speak, and stop an action that our subconscious brain activity primed us for, but wasn't such a good idea when a bit more thought was applied. Our brain also uses our experience and knowledge to predict the best action to take, and because some of our knowledge and experience comes from exercising our limited choices, we can also say we have some input into our decisions.

It's inaccurate and misleading to think of our will being entirely conscious and thought driven.

This has big implications for our mental health. If we believe that we have full conscious control of our thoughts and actions, and we find ourselves in a state of mental distress, then we can get ourselves lost trying to find our way out of the maze; convinced that because it was our choices that got us into trouble, then we should be able to get ourselves out of trouble, if we could only make the right choices.

We can sap our mental energy trying to fight things that are beyond our control, or we can understand that there are some things we need help fixing, and divert our energy into the areas that can be changed for the better.

In the next few chapters, we're going to look at some of the deeper components of our thoughts, feelings and actions so we can start to understand where we can make meaningful change.

3

Thought and the Cognitive Action Pathways Model

Zoolander was one of those cult movies that polarised people into "absolutely love it" or "absolutely loathe it" camps. I admit it, I'm a Zoolander fan.

For those who aren't familiar with the story, Derek Zoolander was a top male model, famous for his different looks: "Blue Steel", "Ferrari", "Le Tigre" and the famous "Magnum". They were all the same pose, of course, but everyone thought they were different. Except for evil fashion designer, Mugatu, who in a burst of rage at the climax of the movie, yells, "Who cares about Derek Zoolander anyway? The man has only one look ... Blue Steel? Ferrari? Le Tigre? They're the same face! Doesn't anybody notice this? I feel like I'm taking crazy pills!"

A model in science is not quite as fun as Zoolander and not ridiculously good looking either, though they are (usually) much smarter. Scientific models are like fashion models in a way, in that they show what something might be like. A scientific model simplifies a complex process to assist with understanding it, and a good scientific model can be used to make accurate predictions.

In the last chapter I described some basic parts of our neurobiology. In this chapter, I'm going to outline a model that shows how I think many of these different pieces work together to explain what goes on under the surface, so to speak. This model will clarify the components that contribute to our complex, creative, cognitive stream.

It may seem a bit too theoretical, but bear with me here. I know that there will be many people reading this book who want practical solutions, but once you have an understanding of what is happening underneath the surface in the depths of our subconscious, it will make mental health conditions much easier to understand, and will help you see why some therapies for mental health problems work, while others are a genuine waste of time. We'll also see how small changes in the deepest part of our biology can radically change the way we perceive and interact with the world.

The Cognitive-Action Pathways Model

The Cognitive-Action Pathways model (or CAP for short) is a way of understanding how our biology influences our subconscious mental processes, which then feed into and influence our conscious stream of thought.

I formulated the model as a way bringing together all of the different strands of neuroscience research that I'd read, and put it in a way that I could better understand. Even though it started off as a tool to help me understand the complexities of our conscious and subconscious processing, I think it also has significant bearing on our understanding of mental health and illness. It shows that small changes in our biology can snowball to create major differences in how we think about and experience the world.[14] By understanding what influences our thoughts and behaviours, we remove unnecessary guilt, form realistic expectations and set attainable goals.

The Cognitive-Action Pathway Model

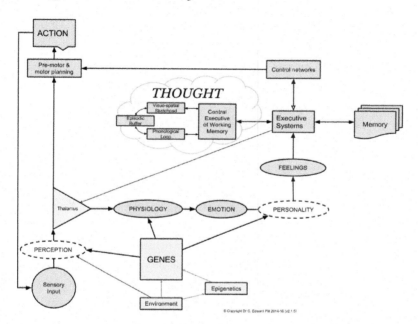

The Cognitive-Action Pathways model is a schematic conceptual representation of the hierarchy of key components that underpin human thought and behaviour

In coming up with the CAP model, I incorporated some well-known and accepted models of cognition, including the Dual Systems Model, and the Cognitive Cycle as described in the Global Workspace/IPA model, as well as concepts not described in other cognitive models, namely the triad of genes, epigenetics and the environment, and the filters of perception and personality.[1]

---

[1] In the interests of full disclosure, I make no specific claim that this model is unique, although I'm unaware of other models incorporating all of these specific elements.

The basic explanation of the CAP model is this: The information received by our senses is processed in many different ways. Habitual or 'reflex' action can take place or the information can be processed by our higher order brain structures. Genes fundamentally influence this by changing how we perceive the information, the way that information alters our physiology, and the bias given by the filter of our personality. This information is combined with long term memories, and processed by our working memory system, which then leads to our actions.

A simple example–CAP in the café

Suppose you're sitting in a café talking to a friend and something lightly brushed the back of your neck.

The sensory input from whatever is lightly brushing your skin is perceived by the touch receptors in the skin. This signal passes to the thalamus where it has to make a rough-and-ready decision about the sensation. It has enough characteristics that make it possible that it's a spider, so the signal goes to the motor areas of the brain and you have a reflexive response to jump out of your chair and brush off whatever it is on the back of your neck. As it turned out it was just the waiter's sleeve brushing against your neck as he walked past, but the first pathway is rough and ready, making reflexive actions quickly without conscious input.

Another simple example

Suppose you're sitting in a café talking to a friend and a man walks up to you, smiles and extends his right hand out to you and says, "Hello".

There are a number of sensory inputs – the vision of the man, his facial and body gestures, and his auditory greeting–which are perceived by your eyes and ears. How your eyes and ears perceives these signals depends on your genes (say, if you've got the genes for colour-blindness) and your environment (like if your ears were blocked with wax, or if you're a bit deaf from too much loud music).

The initial analysis suggests no immediate danger, and your brain starts subconsciously pre-planning possible actions.

Then the signal gets through the gates of physiology and personality which gets filtered and merged into the way you're feeling. How you're feeling then gets passed up with the sensory information to our executive function areas, which have to use those feelings, as well as memory of previous similar situations and their outcomes, and memory of social norms, gestures *et cetera*, to then come up with a set of possible actions, decide on one of them, and send the instructions to other parts of your brain responsible for planning the action and carrying it out.

The usual action: You'd probably stand up, reach out your hand and shake hands with the stranger. It's a social ritual. Even though it seems like a simple action, a lot of processing has gone into it, but that processing is usually very rapid and mostly subconscious.

Let me explain the different components of the system in more detail. In the next chapter, we'll look at a more in-depth example, and come back to the stranger in the café scenario again.

CAP components

There are a number of different influences and subconscious processes that contribute to our stream of conscious awareness.

Genes, epigenetics and the environment

From the simplest bacteria through to all plants, all animals and all of human kind–*EVERY* living thing has DNA. DNA is what defines life in the broadest sense. Genes are fundamental to who we are. Without our genes, we would be nothing more than a salty soup of random amino acids.

Genes provide the code to build proteins. Proteins are responsible for the size, shape and operation of the cell. They make each tissue structurally and functionally different, but still work together in a highly precise electrochemical synchrony.

In order for the right proteins to be made at the right times, the DNA has a number of tags or markers which switch the genes on or off. These tags are called epigenetic markers, and the sequence of epigenetic tags are together called the epigenome.

Environmental factors (the components that make up the world external to our bodies) can influence genes and epigenetic markers. The environment can cause genetic mutations or new epigenetic marks that change the function of a particular gene. The activity of the cell they effect, a very active embryonic cell or a quiet adult cell for example, will largely determine the eventual outcome of that mutation.

The environment and the epigenetic markers are important influences on our genetic expression, but in terms of our resulting phenotype, our genetic code is still the most influential.

Perception

We live in a sensory world. The five senses are vital in providing the input we need for our brain to understand the world and meaningfully interact with it.

We have different organs that translate different forms of energy in our environment into neuronal signals. Eyes translate light into neuronal signals. Ears translate sound waves into neuronal signals. Our skin translates different pressures and heat into neuronal signals. In addition, many chemicals in our environment bind to receptors in our tastebuds and noses, which triggers neuronal signals. Neuronal signals in sensory neurons embedded in our muscles are triggered when they are stretched, which allows us to know where and how our limbs are positioned, even when we are not looking at them. These neuronal signals all travel to different parts of the brain, are processed, and interpreted.

Our genes significantly influence this process. For example, if someone is born with red-green colour blindness, how he or she interprets the world will always be subtly different to someone with normal vision. Or a person born with congenital deafness will always interpret his or her environment in a different way to someone with full hearing. I've highlighted these two conditions because they provide stark examples to help demonstrate the point, but there are many unique genetic expressions in each of our senses that subtly alter the way each of us perceives the world around us.

So while we may all have the same photons of light hitting our retinas, or the same pressure waves of sound reaching our ears or the pressure of touch on our skin, how our brains receive that information is slightly different for every individual. The information from the outside world is *received* by our sensory organs, but it is *perceived* by our brain, and even small differences in perception can have a big impact on the rest of the system.

Personality

Personality is "the combination of characteristics or qualities that form an individual's distinctive character."[15] Formally speaking, personality is, "defined as constitutionally based tendencies in thoughts, behaviors, and emotions that surface early in life, are relatively stable and follow intrinsic paths of development basically independent of environmental influences."[16]

Professor Gregg Henriques explained it well in Psychology Today, "Personality traits are longstanding patterns of thoughts, feelings, and actions which tend to stabilize in adulthood and remain relatively fixed."[17]

In classical psychology, there are five main personality types – 'Neuroticism', 'Extraversion', 'Agreeableness', 'Conscientiousness', and 'Openness to Experience'. Neuroticism, for example, is the sort of person who is pessimistic or 'negative'. They're usually a worrier, easily upset, often down or irritable, and demonstrate high emotional reactivity to stress.[17]

I think of personality as a filter for a camera lens, shaping the awareness of our emotional state for better or worse, thus influencing the flow on to our feelings (the awareness of our emotions), our thoughts, and our actions.

Personality has been suggested to be strongly influenced by the way the serotonin and dopamine chemical signals are handled by our brains.[18-20] In turn, these signals in the brain are strongly influenced by genetic factors, while what we learn outside the home (what researchers term the "non-shared environment") also contributes.[20-25]

Physiology

Physiology refers to the streams of data that are provided from the different parts of your physical body, like heart rate, breathing rate, the oxygen in your blood, the position of your joints, the movement of your joints, even the filling of your bladder telling you that you need a break soon.

Our genes determine our physiology in many different subtle ways on molecular, cellular and tissue levels. One example is that our genes are largely responsible for the baseline function and the response of our adrenal glands when stressed.[26]

All of these signals are constantly being generated, and collated in different parts of the brain. Some researchers consider them positive and negative depending on the data stream and the signal it's providing. They coalesce into emotion.[27]

Emotion

Emotion is a familiar concept in every day life, but surprisingly, the work of literally thousands of brilliant minds has brought us no closer to a scientifically validated definition of the word "emotion". Some psychologists and researchers consider it vague and unscientific, and would prefer that it not be used altogether.[28]

I've retained it because I think it's a well-recognised word that conceptually describes the balance of physiological forces.

According to British doctor and neuroscientist Alan Watkins, "emotion" is the sum of all the data streams of physiology, or what he described as "*E-MOTION ... Energy in MOTION.*"[27]

In this context, think of emotion as a bulls-eye spirit-level of our body systems. The different forces of our physiology change the "level" constantly in different directions. Emotion is the bubble that marks the central point, telling us how far out of balance we are.

Feelings

"Feelings" are the perception of emotion.

I discussed earlier in the chapter that what we perceive is different to what we "see" because the subtle genetic differences in our eyes and brains causes the information to be processed differently between individuals. The same applies to the perception of our emotion.

We know that personality is largely determined by our genetics with contributions from our environment.[24, 25] The emotional signal is filtered by our personality to give rise to our feelings. Classically, an optimistic personality is going to bias the emotional input in an adaptive way while a pessimist or neurotic is going to bias the emotional signal in a maladaptive way.

That's not to say that an optimist can't have depressed feelings, or a neurotic can't have happy feelings. In the same way that a coloured lens will allow a lot of light through but filter certain wavelengths out, most of our emotional state of being will come through the filter of our personality but the feelings will be subtly biased one way or another.

Executive Functions

Executive functions are amazing. They deserve more than one box in my model, but for the sake of simplicity, one box is all they get.

Executive functions are the central hub of information processing, taking the incoming signals and figuring out what to do with them. They're complex cognitive processes, with the co-ordination of several sub-processes required to achieve a particular goal.[29] These sub-processes can be variable but include working memory, attention, goal setting, maintaining and monitoring of our action telling us when to stop.

Executive functions process the incoming information and decide on what goals are best given the context, then plan the goals, execute them to the motor cortices, and monitor the action.

Executive functions are almost always subconscious. Some memories, and the function of working memory tends to be conscious – in other words, we're aware of the thoughts and memories that are involved in some of our executive functions, but a lot of goals and actions are formed below the surface, without our conscious awareness.

Research work from a group of scientists led by Professor Marien demonstrates that subconscious goals can divert resources away from conscious goals especially if it is emotionally important or otherwise strongly related. They also confirm that conscious awareness is not necessary for executive function but that implicit goals can be formed and executed without conscious involvement.[30] In other words, your brain can decide what it needs to do, and then do it without you ever being aware of what was going on underneath.

Thoughts

I discussed the science of thought in the section 'Components of Consciousness' in the previous chapter. I won't go over it all again here, but the key points for the CAP model are that thought is made up of the different sub-systems which we 'hear' and 'see' in our mind.

We are consciously aware of the information as it's projected from other parts of our brain into our working memory. Our stream of thought is made up of a number of cognitive cycles running several times a second which we see as a continuous flow of information, just like we see a movie as continuous even though it's a series of still images.

Action

Action is the final step in the process—the output, our tangible behaviour.

Our behaviour is not always the direct result of conscious thought, or our will (as considered in the sense of our conscious will). It might be a reflexive action caused by the subconscious rough-and-ready assessment of our deeper brain structures like our thalamus. Often times it's an automatic script or previously learned set of actions that has been utilised by the implicit goals and motivations that our subconscious executive functions have assessed as the best course of action.

If it is to become part of our conscious experience, information has proceeded from our sensory input through our perceptions, tagged with our physiology and coalesced into an emotion, which is filtered by our personality to render a feeling. This is combined with our previous memories and implicit goals, and if necessary, fed into our working memory. Nearly all of this process is influenced by our genes and their expression.

Once our working memory has processed the information, it's fed back into our executive functions to make a final decision. There's an element of awareness that provides real-time monitoring and a veto function, but most of the time, we're not fully conscious of every action we make, although our brains give us the impression that we are.

Summary

The Cognitive-Action Pathways model is a way of describing the relationship of our thoughts to other biological and cognitive processes.

It shows that conscious thoughts are a single link within a much longer chain of neurological functions between stimulus and action—simply one cog in the machine.

This chapter was about setting out the place that our thoughts have in the grand scheme of life. It's not a plug for genetic pre-determination. We are not a victim of our genes, but at the same time, we are not the master and commander either.

In the next chapter, I'll show how the CAP model can apply using a real-world example, Autism Spectrum Disorder. The autism spectrum provides a good example of how changes in genes and their expression can dramatically influence every aspect of a person's life—how they experience the world, how they feel about those experiences, and how they think about them.

4

The CAP in action

In the last chapter, I explained the Cognitive-Action Pathways model (or CAP for short), a way of representing the pathways that form the basis of our thoughts and actions.

The CAP model shows that, from our genes all the way up to our memories and experiences, there's a complex interplay of biology which results in our actions. Our biology strongly influences how we perceive information, how we process that information and how we combine that information into our memories of the past, predictions of the future, and our understanding of the present.[14]

A real life example of this is ASD, or Autism Spectrum Disorder. We'll discuss ASD in a more clinical sense in a later chapter, but the purpose of this chapter is to use ASD as an example of how the CAP model applies to real life. ASD is an excellent example of the CAP model in action, because autism gives a clear example of small changes in a number of genes can snowball to affect every other part of the process.

A brief primer on autism

ASD has been present since time immemorial. Autism used to be considered a form of demon possession, madness or schizophrenia. Some early therapists thought it was caused by emotionally distant "refrigerator mothers". Poor understanding of autism lead to inhumane experimental "treatments."[31, 32]

Thankfully we have a much better understanding of autism in our modern day and age. The autism spectrum is defined by two main characteristics: deficits in social communication and interaction, and restricted repetitive patterns of behaviour. People on the autism spectrum also tend to have abnormal sensitivity to stimuli, and are more likely to suffer from co-existing conditions like ADHD.

One more important definition: in the ASD community, "neurotypical" is the word given to describe the person without autism (some people would say, "Why not just call a neurotypical person 'normal'", but that would imply that those with autism are abnormal, so neurotypical is the better word to use).

The CAP model in ASD

Genetics

According to the CAP model, changes in our genetics have effects that carry all the way up the chain to affect our thoughts and our actions.

This is clearly seen in autism. Twin studies suggest that between 70-90% of the risk of autism is genetic.[33, 34] The increased genetic risk of autism doesn't arise from one or two big mutations but from hundreds of different genes that are either over-expressed or under-expressed.[35, 36]

Epigenetics and the environment

There are a few environmental factors that have a smaller effect on the development of autism. These include disorders of folate metabolism,[37, 38] pollutants,[39] fever during pregnancy[40] and medications such as valproate and certain anti-depressants[41, 42] that are linked with an increase in autism.[2] Supplements such as folate,[37, 43] omega-6 polyunsaturated fatty acids[44] and the use of paracetamol for fevers in pregnancy[40] have protective effects.

The combined effect of genes, environment and epigenetics

The abnormal gene expression changes the function of parts of the cell's machinery that hobble the ability of the nerve cell to fully develop, and the ability of nerve cells to form connections with other nerve cells[34, 45]

This means that in the brain of an unborn baby that will develop ASD, excess numbers of dysfunctional nerve cells are unable to form the correct synaptic scaffolding, leaving a brain that is large but out-of-sync.[46, 47] The reduced scaffolding leads to local over-connectivity within regions of the brain, and under-connectivity between the regions of the brain.[35]

To put this into a more concrete example, think of a big city. A normal city has lots of small roads connecting the houses in a suburb, and much larger roads connecting the suburbs. Now imagine a city that had the opposite – arterial roads and freeways between the houses in each suburb, and narrow two lanes roads between the suburbs. You could move really quickly and easily house to house, but it would be really hard to drive from suburb to suburb. That's what the autistic brain is like.

---

[2] A word of caution: While there's good evidence that valproate increases the risk of autism, and a possible link between some anti-depressants and autism, that risk has to be balanced with the risk to the baby of having a mother with uncontrolled epilepsy or depression, which may very well be higher. If you're taking these medications and you're pregnant, or you want to become pregnant, consult your doctor BEFORE you stop or change your medications. Work out what's right for you (and your baby) in your unique situation.

In ASD, the majority of the abnormal cells and connections are within the frontal lobe, especially the dorsolateral prefrontal cortex and the medial prefrontal cortex,[48] as well as the temporal lobes.[49] The cerebellum is also significantly linked to the autism spectrum.[50] There is also evidence that the amygdala and hippocampus, involved in emotional regulation and memory formation, are significantly effected in ASD.[35]

There is also strong evidence for an over-active immune system in an autistic person compared to a neurotypical person, with changes demonstrated in all parts of the immune system, in both the brain and the rest of the body.[51] These immune changes contribute to the reduced ability of the brain to form new branches as well as develop new nerve cells or remove unnecessary cells.

The effects on sensory input

These changes in the structure of the ASD brain, the local over-connection and the distant under-connection, cause a flow-on effect to the way information is processed. According to the CAP model these changes influence perception, physiology and personality.

Perception

The brain processes sound in the temporal lobes, which are located on both sides of the brain, just above each ear. Language processing, which is a special type of sound analysis, is usually done on the left side of the brain, with some effect from the right side. Normally the left side processes words, while the right side processes the non-verbal parts of language, like the rhythm and tone of speech, as well as non-speech sounds. In people with autism, because of the abnormal wiring, there is only significant activity of the right temporal lobe.[49]

Research has shown that newborn babies from as young as two days old prefer listening to their own native language, which suggests that we're born already pre-wired for language. What's amazing is that studies have been able to show that babies have specific brain activity in their left temporal lobe when their name is spoken compared to other words or to random non-speech noises.[52]

In an ASD brain, however, the change in the wiring of the left and right temporal lobes alters the processing of language, which results in a reversing of the brain's orientation to social and non-social sounds. In other words, the brain of a baby with ASD will respond the same to their name, to a random word, or to a non-speech sound like the sound of a bell.[53] So already from a young age, people with autism will respond differently to environmental stimuli compared to a neurotypical person.

In the same way, brain changes in a person with ASD alters the way they process faces. The fusiform gyrus is part of the brain that processes faces. It's normally quite specific to this task. The altered wiring of the brain in someone with autism causes a change, with different parts of the brain having to take up the load of facial processing.[54] This means that a person with ASD can't process all the different nuances of facial expressions that are part of normal body language.

Depending on what study you read, non-verbal communication (body language, facial expressions, and the rhythm and tone of the speech) make up between 50-90% of communication. Because of the changes to the processing of language and faces found in ASD, people with autism miss at least half the message.

Imagine a neurotypical person and an autistic person both standing in front of their boss. They may be listening to the same words, and seeing the same facial expressions, but because of the way each person's brain processes the information, the message they receive can be completely different, which can dramatically effect how they do at their job, whether they get promoted, or whether they even keep their job.

Physiology

The incorrect synaptic scaffolding, and the out-of-sync neural networks also change the wiring of deeper brain structures like the amygdala.

The amygdala is larger in young children with ASD compared to typically developing children. As a result, young ASD children have higher levels of background anxiety than do neurotypical children.[55] It's proposed that not only do ASD children have higher levels of background anxiety, they also have more difficulty in regulating their stress system, resulting in higher levels of stress compared to a neurotypical child exposed to the same situation.[56]

Personality

On a chemical level, autism involves genes that encode for proteins involved in the transport of some key neurotransmitters, mainly serotonin and dopamine. Early evidence confirms the deficits of the serotonin and dopamine transporter systems in autism.[57]

The decreased ability of serotonin and dopamine to relay messages means that occurrences that should be rewarding or comforting are much less so. This changes how stress and rewards are interpreted. People with ASD naturally tend to exaggerate stress and underestimate rewards, which in turn, makes them more likely to be more pessimistic and introverted.[58, 59] Their feelings, their thoughts and their resulting actions are tinged by the differences in personality through which all of the incoming signals are processed.

Memory

Again, the incorrect synaptic scaffolding, and the out-of-sync neural networks cause changes in deep brain structures like the hippocampus and cerebellum.

The hippocampus is largely responsible for transforming working memory into longer-term declarative memory. Studies comparing the size of the hippocampus in ASD children have shown an increase in size compared with typical developing children.[60] Combined with the deficits in the nerve cell structure of the cerebellum,[50] autistic children and adults have a poor procedural memory (action learning, regulated by the cerebellum) and an overdeveloped declarative memory (for facts, regulated by the hippocampus). This has been termed the "Mnesic Imbalance Theory."[61]

Actions

The cerebellum isn't just involved in procedural memory, but also in co-ordination of fine movements.[50, 62] So people on the autism spectrum have differences in the way they perform their actions, not just on deciding what those actions will be.

The cerebellum in a person with ASD has reduced numbers of a particular cell called the Purkinje cells, effecting the output of the cerebellum and the refined co-ordination of the small muscles of the hands (amongst other things). Reduced co-ordination of the fine motor movements of the hands means that handwriting is less precise and therefore less neat.

When Hans Asperger first described his cohort of ASD children, he noted that they all had a tendency to be clumsy and have poor handwriting.[63]

A running joke when I talk to people is the notoriously illegible doctors handwriting. I tell people that our handwriting is terrible because we spent six years at medical school having to take notes at 200 words a minute.

But then again, it might also be that the qualities that make for a good doctor tend to be found in Asperger's Syndrome (excellent memory for facts, obsessive tendencies etc), so the medical school selection process is going to bias the cohort of medical students towards ASD and the associated poor handwriting (Thankfully, those that go on to neurosurgery tend to have good hand-eye coordination).

If your educational experience was anything like mine, handwriting was seen as one of the key performance indicators of school life. If your handwriting was poor, you were considered lazy or stupid. Even excluding the halo effect from the equation, poor handwriting means a student has to slow down to write more neatly but takes longer to complete the same task, or write faster to complete the task in the allotted time but sacrificing legibility in doing so.

Either way, the neurobiology of ASD results in reduced ability to effectively communicate, leading to judgement from others and internal personal frustration, both of which feedback to the level of personality, moulding future feelings, thoughts and actions.

Thought in ASD

By the time all the signals have gone through the various layers of perception, personality and physiology, they reach the conscious awareness level of our stream of thought. While thoughts are as unique as the individual that thinks them, the common genetic expression of ASD and the resulting patterns in personality, physiology and perception lead to some predictable patterns of thought in those sharing the same genes.

As a consequence of the differences in the signal processing, the memories that make their way to long-term storage are also going to be different. Memories and memory function are also different in ASD for other neurobiological reasons, as described earlier in the chapter with the Mnesic Imbalance Theory.

Back to the man in the café ...

In the last chapter, I used an example of the CAP model at work in an everyday situation. Knowing what we know about ASD and the CAP model now, how does the stranger in the café situation change for a person on the spectrum?

There are a number of sensory inputs – the vision of the man, his facial expressions and body gestures, and his auditory greeting.

Perception of these sensory inputs is different because of changes in how the brain is wired – a person on the spectrum has difficulty processing social cues such as facial expressions and tone and rhythm of speech. So for the person on the spectrum, much of the information from the stranger's facial expressions and body language is missed.

In someone with ASD, their amygdala is larger and more active, so the fact that a stranger has walked up to them has already set off danger signals, which has activated the adrenaline system. Their physiology is primed, with muscles tightening, heart rate beating faster, and stomach suddenly feeling a lot more sensitive.

People on the ASD spectrum also tend to have neurotic personalities—pessimistic and untrusting. So the combination of perception, physiology and personality is a feeling of anxiety and mistrust, with no body language cues to assuage them.

This feeling of anxiety then gets passed up with the sensory information to the executive function areas. The person on the spectrum has to then process the current situation and sense of anxiety with previous experiences, memories, and training, and come up with a set of possible actions, decide on one of them, and carry it out.

For the person on the spectrum, a lot of brain power is being utilised here, compared with the neurotypical person where very little thought would be required. The person on the spectrum is using up a lot of conscious thought power, trying to understand the motives of this stranger, and suppress their overwhelming anxiety, before they feebly stick out their hand and quickly shake it, uncomfortable because of their anxiety and touch hypersensitivity, unable to maintain eye contact because they feel overwhelmed.

This is why people on the autism spectrum look so odd. It's one of the most basic social interactions, and while a neurotypical person would do it easily, the person on the spectrum hesitates and looks awkward, shakes hands insipidly, and has no eye contact.

And it's all because of the abnormal expression of a number of genes, feeding up the chain of information processing within the subconscious depths of our brains.

Summary

Our thoughts, feelings, personality, and behaviour – all the elements that form the basis of our mental health – are determined by our biology interacting with the external environment that we individually experience.

I used autism as an example for this chapter because autism is a condition that touches every aspect of a person's life, and provides a good example of the extensive consequences from small genetic changes.

The same principles of the Cognitive-Action Pathways Model apply to all aspects of life, including conditions that are considered pathological, but also to our normal variations and idiosyncrasies. Small variations in the genes that code for our smell sensors or the processing of smells can change our preferences for certain foods just as much as cultural exposure. Our appreciation for music is often changed subtly between individuals because of small changes in the structure of our ears or the nerves that we use to process the sounds. The genetic structure of the melanin pigment in our skin changes our interaction with our environment because of the amount of exposure to the sun we can handle.

I wanted to explain the CAP model in detail to explain why I believe that mental health, and therefore mental illness, is not only a direct result of our personal choices as is popularly believed. This is important to understand because if we focus on the wrong causes of mental illness, we'll also focus on the wrong treatments. After all, why waste precious time and energy (and money) on trying to fix the things that we don't have any tools yet to fix. We should focus on the parts that we can fix.

We'll discuss more about this in the next chapter.

5

Acceptance, Understanding and Serenity

Einstein is credited with saying, "Everybody is a genius. But if you judge a fish by its ability to climb a tree, it will live its whole life believing that it is stupid."

It's a great quote; notwithstanding the minor discrepancies that: (1) not everyone's a genius, and (2) Einstein didn't actually say it.[64] Inaccuracies aside, the point the quote is making is still mostly true. Unrealistic expectations about someone or something make for failure and disappointment for all concerned.

In John 8:32, Jesus said, "... you shall know the truth, and the truth shall set you free". As Christians, we know that Jesus was speaking words of profound spiritual guidance. There's also truth to this statement at a more general level, however, because when you understand what's really going on, you're free.

Imagine you're stuck in a maze. With wrong directions, or with no directions, you face hours of fruitless wandering and frustration. You're trapped. When you have the right directions, you're free to navigate out of the maze and you're liberated.

The same metaphor applies to thoughts and actions. We all have behaviours that we don't like, and that we want to change. Sometimes we can change them ourselves, but other times, we find ourselves stuck in a pattern of unwanted thoughts, feelings or behaviours, and as hard as we try, we still remain trapped. We get stuck, unable to move through the maze, frustratingly trying over and over again to find our way out, only to find ourselves back where we started.

If you happened to be trapped in a maze, the most useful thing to have would be a map, or at least someone with a map that could help navigate. The wrong directions, or no directions, guarantee more failure, but the right directions give hope, and eventually, freedom. That's what this chapter is all about: Hope, freedom, and finding the right path.

In the last chapter I used autism as an example of how the Cognitive-Action Pathways Model works in a real life. The model doesn't just apply to autism, but for all of our thoughts and actions in all aspects of our lives. In this chapter, I want to explain how the Cognitive-Action Pathways model can be applied to other parts of our lives – in our everyday lives and in mental illness.

It's by understanding the relationships of our actions to our thoughts and to the rest of our biology that we see the right steps, get the right directions, and finally free ourselves from the maze. At the same time, we can remove the weight of guilt and disappointment that unrealistic expectations cause us.

Remember: Truth resulting in hope and freedom via the right path – they're our goals.

Genes, environment and pre-determination

The popular media and some pop psychologists can give us conflicting opinions about the battle of nature and nurture. In the early 20th century, eugenics was a powerful philosophy, and much of society approved of the notion of controlled breeding to increase the occurrence of desirable heritable characteristics. Eugenics was based on the idea that genes were solely responsible for physical traits. The pendulum swung away from the determinism of genes in the 1940's as psychiatrists moved to the behaviourism model promoted by B.F. Skinner. The pendulum of public opinion swung back towards the absolute determinism of genes in the late 20th century as new scientific discoveries saw gene mutations as the cause of disease.

In reality, both genes AND the environment make us who we are. It's wrong to think that our genes control us completely, just as it's wrong to say our genes have no effect at all.

In modern research, biologists have studied the question of the influence of nature (genes) versus nurture (the environment) with GxE studies, shorthand for Gene x Environment. Using the best available data involving large numbers of people with a particular trait and without it, common gene variations are analysed and the average effect of those genes is compared to the influence of the environment. The result is expressed as a percentage split. For example, 88% of the chance that a person will develop insulin dependent diabetes is related to their genes, while the remaining 12% is determined by their environment.[65] On a population level, the power of genes and the environment can be averaged, and shown by GxE studies, but the genetic risk for an individual is unique because different mutations, polymorphisms and variants each have their own unique levels of expression.

So genes have a significant impact on our biology but they don't have the final say in everything. Genes are like a set of corrals, limiting the area in which we have the power to choose.

Take a couple of obvious examples: my genes determine my gender and my athletic ability. I can partially determine the effect over one genetic trait but I can never change the other. That is, if I worked supremely hard, I could run a five-minute mile, but no matter how hard I tried, I can't change my biological gender (I could take hormones that would give me a female appearance, but I could never change my XY chromosomes, become pregnant or give birth).

So either way my genes limit my choices, at least to some extent. One set of genes dictates some absolute limits (my gender, and my ability to get pregnant). The other set of genes provides a limit that I could eventually overcome (my athletic ability), but it would take a lot of hard work, which still limits my ultimate decisions.

This is important for two reasons: 1. We still have some choices, but 2. We can only change what's changeable.

Whatever your family history or genetic lineage is, it doesn't completely negate personal choice. You may have a higher risk of an illness because of your lineage, but you can engage in appropriate therapy to help negate that risk, though sometimes you do everything right to prevent an unwanted trait and it occurs anyway. You can't control everything.

For example, you may have a genetic risk of depression of 66%. With the right tools, you may halve your risk, which is good going by any standards. But that still leaves you with a 33% chance of suffering depression, and if you end up being the one out of three, there's no shame in it.

There was a study published in the prestigious medical journal Lancet in 2001. This study looked at people with pre-diabetes, who through lifestyle modification (i.e.: radically changing their environment), managed to achieve an average 58% reduction in their risk of developing diabetes. Still, after four years, 11% of them developed diabetes anyway.[66] This is a good example of how choices can *sometimes* change your ultimate destiny.

So I'll say it again, because this is important. Genes don't completely negate your power to choose, but they set limits over what choices you can make, and they also still have a say in the final outcome of your choices.

Thought in its proper place

Placing your thoughts at the top of the chain as the most influential step in the process is like placing the Earth in the centre of the Solar System. It seems intuitively correct. Aristotle declared that the Earth is stationary and must be the centre of the universe, because the Earth doesn't seem to move, rather, everything else moves around us. In the same way, Descartes mused, "I think, therefore I am", noting how our thoughts are so integral to our being that they must be the centre of it.

Aristotle's view disabled scientific reasoning and discovery for centuries until Copernicus proposed the view that the Earth wasn't central, but was actually the third planet circling the central sun.

In the same way, by getting thought in its proper place, everything else in the process aligns and enables us to move forward purposefully. We see that thought is dependent on a number of steps beyond our conscious influence.

This puts the "helpful" advice that we get from other people into perspective. Like medical doctor and neuroscientist Alan Watkins observed in his TEDx presentation, "So if you feel anxious, for example, it's no good me saying to you, 'Don't worry.' You'll have experienced that doesn't work."[27]

How often do your friends tell you, "Don't worry", or you say the same to them? It's fairly redundant, because no matter how much they say it, it doesn't stop you from worrying.

Mistakenly elevating the power of thought about everything else only produces feelings of frustration, guilt and failure. My son loves the show, "Mythbusters". One episode[67] tested some "Battle of the Sexes" myths, one of them being the idea that men don't ask for directions when they get lost. They took ten men and ten women, put them in the middle of suburbia without a map, and gave them a misleading set of directions. The result was, of course, that all twenty volunteers got lost.

The reactions of the volunteers provided some interesting insights. They all drove around trying to retrace their steps, trying to figure out where they went wrong, trying not to look stupid on an internationally broadcast TV show. The more they drove around, the more lost they became. They all got frustrated. You could see their anxiety rising as each time they tried to go back to their starting point in the endless maze of uniformly bland streets and houses, they would find themselves driving around in circles. The men did this for an average of four whole minutes; the women did it for over five minutes. Two of the volunteers drove completely lost for a full fifteen minutes before the hosts pulled them off the course to put them out of their misery.

It didn't matter how hard they tried, either to follow the (incorrect) instructions better, or try and rely on their own skills. They didn't find their way to their desired location until they asked the "neighbours" (people planted around the streets by the producers) to give them directions.

Thoughts are much the same. If you try and fix your thought pattern with 'better' thinking, you'll wind up confused, frustrated and entirely stuck. It's no good telling yourself or someone else to "just try harder", or "stop thinking toxic thoughts" or "just be a better person" or anything else for that matter.

Admittedly the surge of hope that accompanies self-help mantras and pop-psychology does make you feel better for a while, a bit like the first four days of a diet. But they inevitably lead to a crash because they're trying to fix dysfunctional thinking with dysfunctional thinking, essentially trying to fix the symptom not the cause. These repeated failures reinforce feelings of guilt, shame or the despair of failure, and often cause guilt about having guilt, or anxiety over having anxiety.

Having thought in its proper place makes it easy to understand why pop psychology and self-help mantras don't work. It also allows you to make changes that realign the upstream processes so that the important outcomes like awareness and actions are aligned with your values.

What about choices?

As I said before, our genes have a corralling effect, limiting some choices, but allowing enough space in others that to overcome them by efficient effort and determination.

Choices that make lasting changes relate to two things: Action and Feedback.

Modern psychological therapies like Acceptance and Commitment Therapy confirm that behavioural activation trumps cognitive restructuring, or in other words, life change comes from changing your actions not changing your thoughts. Improvement comes with better coaching, a principle that applies as much to the sporting field as it does to life in general.

Like the volunteers on Mythbusters, when they stopped and asked someone else for the right directions, their frustration and confusion stopped and they found their way out of their maze. If you want to find your way out of your own maze of frustration and confusion, take action. Find someone who can provide the right solutions, ask for their help, and push forward to fulfil your values.

Whatever actions we choose, we automatically acquire feedback through our sensory input (our senses). Whatever the action is, all of the senses are involved in receiving data so that the action can be encoded, correlated and stored as our brains build a database of knowledge for future use.

In modern psychology, this feedback loop is known as Operant Learning, first formally described by the pioneering behavioural psychologist B. F. Skinner in the 1950's, but it has always been an integral part of the basic human experience.

This operant learning feedback loop acts in two ways within the context of our personal choices. Firstly, we learn the positive consequences of desired actions, which can have the effect of correcting our unhelpful thought process. When we act according to our new set of instructions and the predictions of our maladaptive thinking don't materialise as we expected, new memories are stored. These new memories influence how we make future decisions while encouraging more of the same actions. Secondly, the flipside is also true, in that we can learn the unwanted outcomes of unhelpful actions, and not perform them in the future.

Bringing it all together

When it all boils down to basics, this model is about understanding and empowerment.

Understanding: because we all need to recognise what it is about ourselves that we can't change, what we can change, and what we need to change. We all have parts of us that we can't change, or that we could change if we wanted to, but that would not have a great impact on the quality of our lives. Understanding the parts of our lives that are both amenable and critical is the key to life change.

Empowerment: because when you recognise what it is about your life that you can't change, you stop wasting precious strength and time fighting it. Instead, all of the effort that would have been needlessly spent on the unchangeable can be effectively spent on improving what needs to be, and can be, changed.

In the last chapter, I used autism as an example of how small changes to a person's genetic information can flow through to effect nearly everything about how they experience life.

A person with high functioning autism (Aspergers Syndrome, to use the old classification) could spend their whole life trying to change themselves to be "more normal". But rather than fighting to change their perception or their personality or their underlying physiology, a more effective strategy is to understand they will always have some oversensitivity to certain sensory stimuli. They may have a tendency to be more anxious. They may be more inclined to miss some social cues. They will be more literal, more analytical, and more concrete than other people.

By pulling out of the needless, endless struggle with things that can't be changed, they can move forward onto things that can be changed. They can be coached in social skills, giving them more confidence.

More knowledge and confidence naturally eases anxiety. When anxiety inevitably arises, they can accept it and use the skills of basic meditation to reduce it. As a result of focusing on effective action, they have improved their quality of life without changing who they are.

The model applies to other physical and mental health problems too. Do you, or have you suffered from depression? You're in good company: great historical leaders such as Winston Churchill and Abraham Lincoln, performers like Kylie and Danii Minogue, and funny men like Jim Carrey and Zach Braff, have all suffered from depression. It can be difficult to see anything other than despair, but trying to fight negative thinking doesn't help, and often increases the struggle. Instead, taking that first action-step slows, then reverses the downward momentum, even if it is simply going for a walk or sharing your despair with a health professional.

Perhaps you're frustrated by a bad habit? Frustration is common because bad habits seem so hard to break, but is your habit really "bad"? So what if you chew your nails or scratch yourself? Those things don't define your self worth. If they aren't harming you in any way, why try and fight them?

Perhaps you smoke? Smoking isn't good for you, to be sure, but it doesn't make you a bad person or unworthy of love or joy. Your genetic background increases your risk of starting, and reduces your chances of stopping, and by understanding that, you can be prepared for the fight ahead. The flipside to understanding that quitting is tough is to realistically frame your progress. Slow progress doesn't mean you're weak. Quite the opposite – acting on the choices that you do have and overcoming, even if it's slow and difficult, actually shows that you are stronger. The key is to seek advice and take that first step. Value-directed action is powerful and results in life change even if your thoughts don't change.

The most poetic of summaries

The Cognitive-Action Pathways model, modern neurobiology and modern psychology help us approach our state of health in a scientific way.

Though decades before science cottoned on, a prayer was published that so neatly summarises the process of acceptance, change, values and mindfulness that it may as well be the prototype model for life enhancement.

Shortly after it became published, it was officially adopted by Alcoholics Anonymous, and has assisted millions of people around the world as part of numerous mutual aid fellowships. Although it was not officially titled when it was first published, it has become known as the Serenity Prayer.

God, give me grace to accept with serenity
the things that cannot be changed,
Courage to change the things
which should be changed,
and the Wisdom to distinguish
the one from the other.
Living one day at a time,
Enjoying one moment at a time,
Accepting hardship as a pathway to peace,
Taking, as Jesus did,
This sinful world as it is,
Not as I would have it,
Trusting that You will make all things right,
If I surrender to Your will,
So that I may be reasonably happy in this life,
And supremely happy with You forever in the next.

Amen.

Final remarks

Every two-bit life coach and pop-psychologist has some quasi-realistic seven-step process. Most of them are useless. Some manage to marginally out-perform the placebo effect, but usually they're the ones that through sheer luck, provide some behavioural therapy somewhere along the line.

Ultimately, thought is nothing more than the projection of a small part of the much larger information cycle within the brain, a single section of music within the grand symphony. Incorrectly assuming thought to be the conductor diverts attention away from the bigger picture, and targets the wrong part with the wrong solutions. Putting thought back in its proper place ensures that meaningful action can take place.

Like the Mythbusters episode, trying to find your way out of a maze with the wrong instructions eventually results in frustration and confusion. Understanding the parts of our lives that are important and amenable to change, and focusing our effort on those things, not wasting our time fighting things that aren't important or aren't yet amenable to change, stops the frustration and confusion.

In the next chapter, we're going to look at a revolutionary perspective that incorporates these principles of acceptance and committed action according to our values.

6

F.A.C.T.

We all want to live a fulfilling and productive life.

The trouble is, most people aren't sure how.

As a result, self-help books are now an 11-billion-dollar industry, as people look for ways to improve their life and find the meaning and fulfilment that they seem to be missing. Christians aren't immune to this phenomenon. Rick Warren's "The Purpose Driven Life" has sold more than 32 million copies since 2002, topping the New York Times best-sellers list at its peak.

Whether it's fulfilment through self-improvement, or finding your purpose in God, the numbers don't lie... mankind is desperate for a richer and more meaningful life.

Except, it seems, that we haven't found it yet.

Despite the plethora of self-help books, our constantly improving standard of living, and our never-ending quests to find happiness and fulfilment, it seems that we're not happy at all as a society.

Why? Clearly we're missing something that's not found in most self-help books and personal development courses.

The answer is actually right in front of us. The reason why we're all so dissatisfied is because we're all trying so hard to avoid being dissatisfied.

And the more we try and strive for happiness, the more miserable we become.

That seems a little counter-intuitive doesn't it? The problem lies in human nature. We naturally try to avoid physical pain, and we think the same applies for life as well. That is, if we want to be happy, we need to avoid feelings and emotions that are uncomfortable or painful – those so called "negative emotions" or "toxic thoughts". Christians have been particularly vulnerable to this teaching.

Why there's no such thing as 'toxic' thoughts

1. Our brain is designed to think 'negative' thoughts

There are two big problems with making 'toxic' thoughts into the Boogey Monster.

First of all, our brain is designed to think 'negative' thoughts. That's how God created us.

The brain is our "don't get killed" organ. It's wired for our survival. It does this in a couple of ways: (1) it looks for danger and plans ways to avoid or escape from it, and (2) it helps us live together with other humans in groups.

Adam and Eve may not have needed to use this neural circuitry initially, but from the moment they were banished from the Garden of Eden, they and every descendent of theirs needed a brain wired for survival.

Think of a time in human-kind's ancient history. Those people living on the savannah who assumed that the rustling of the bush was just the wind instead of realising it was a wild animal would end up being lunch. Being constantly alert to danger was necessary. Without those constant assessments of threat and planning for the possibility of danger, you were more likely to end up dead.

The other thing that aided survival was the ability to remain part of your tribe. If you were excluded from your tribe for whatever reason, you'd either starve, or again, become lunch for some predator. Those who were able to plan ways of staying useful to the tribe would survive longer, so the brain is also naturally wired to constantly compare how useful you are to other people, and to do whatever's necessary to fit in.

In the last 200 years, Western society has gone through a radical transformation. Our tribes are different, our predators and food sources are different, but our brains remain much the same. Our brains are still looking for danger and planning ways to escape from it, and they're still comparing ourselves to others in our "tribe," trying to stay useful.

So thoughts like, "I'm not good enough" or feelings of shame or embarrassment are simply your brains normal wiring to help you stay part of the tribe. Feelings of anxiety or fear, or thoughts of "I can't do that" are often your brains warning signals trying to keep you from danger and to keep you alive. Some would say these thoughts and feelings are 'negative' or 'toxic' but they're not 'toxic' at all—they're normal thoughts and feelings with an adaptive function.

2. Doing positive things requires 'negative' thoughts and feelings

The other problem with the 'toxic' thoughts theory is that doing positive things requires 'negative' thoughts and feelings.

Think for a moment of anything successful you've ever done. Maybe it was an amazing speech you gave, or asking that special someone out on your first date, or winning a race, or winning a grand final with your team, or performing or producing an amazing theatrical or musical performance ... anything that you've done that's been deeply satisfying, pleasurable or elating has probably also been accompanied by uncomfortable feelings. The anxiety you felt before you popped the question to your true love, or the pain involved in the training for the race or the sporting match, the hours you spent learning lines or practicing your instrument so you could perform at your best and get that standing ovation at the end. Everything in life that's fulfilling and enriching is also accompanied by those feelings of discomfort, anxiety, stress or just plain hard work.

Disconnection and dissatisfaction

And so the general dissatisfaction that most people have in life comes from this disconnection—they want happiness, satisfaction, richness and fulfilment but they don't want the discomfort that is inevitably part of the processes. The old psychology and the teachings based on it suggest that if we fight or suppress the discomfort or the 'negative' thoughts, then 'positive' emotions will magically take their place.

About 20 years ago, a psychologist in the USA called Steven Hayes proposed that our psyche was largely built on our arbitrary use of words, which he termed "Relational Frame Theory." Coming from that, he and his colleagues developed Acceptance and Commitment Therapy.

Relational Frame Theory and ACT propose that most of our unhappiness in life stems from the arbitrary values that we apply to words and concepts. Rather than having to fight the unpleasant thoughts or feelings that inevitably arise in life, we should reframe them by considering them for what they really are—simply words and feelings that are meant to be there. We then need to allow them space, and focus instead on taking values-based action, which is the true source of meaning and fulfilment in our lives.

ACT was never meant to have any spiritual connections. A number of people see similarities with ACT and some Buddhist practices, though the creator of the ACT framework specifically denies that it was influenced by any particular religion. When I learnt the ACT framework for the first time, it was as a spiritually neutral psychological treatment. The more I read about and used the ACT framework, however, the more I realised that the Bible has already given us the ACT framework through its various teaching. Indeed, salvation, the crux of our entire life of faith, is essentially an ACT-based process.

What is ACT?

First of all, what is ACT? Acceptance and Commitment Therapy, known as 'ACT' (pronounced as the word 'act') is "a mindfulness based behavioural therapy that challenges the ground rules of most Western psychology. It utilizes an eclectic mix of metaphor, paradox, and mindfulness skills, along with a wide range of experiential exercises and values-guided behavioural interventions."[68]

Traditional psychology heavily relied on CBT (Cognitive-Behavioural Therapy). CBT taught people that in order to be able to take effective action, you had to first conquer the negative thought patterns that were holding you back. It's from this simple premise that Western pop-psychology has its roots. Negative thoughts hold us back; positive thoughts propel us forward. If we think positive, we will be positive, and our lives will be successful, rich and powerful. If we think negatively, we will be negative, and our lives will be pathetic, sad and empty.

ACT is ground-breaking, and is considered the driving force of the new wave of psychological therapies. Unlike traditional and pop-psychology,

ACT teaches that it's immaterial whether our thoughts are 'positive' or 'negative', but that success is a meaningful life based on our values, and that unpleasant feelings and emotions are an inevitable part of that:

"The goal of ACT is to create a rich and meaningful life, while accepting the pain that inevitably goes with it ... taking effective action guided by our deepest values and in which we are fully present and engaged."[68]

I'm not the world's greatest actor, but I've performed a number of times in different churches and community plays. A couple of years ago, I was lucky enough to be involved in a Christmas musical for the church I was attending. I'd had a break from performing for about 15 years to finish medical school and to get through my post-graduate training, so I was rusty to say the least! I was offered the part of the Narrator, and when I got the script, I had a minor conniption. There were pages and pages of dialogue that I had to learn, including several monologues.

The next three months were very challenging. There was a lot of work involved, not just in learning a third of the script word for word, but I also had to learn new performance skills and a dance for the finale (I'm NOT a good dancer!!) When we did each of the performances for real, I was insanely nervous. My heart raced, my muscles all tightened, I was sweating, and I paced for an hour before each performance, worried that I was going to forget my lines. But in the end, when it was all finished and I took my final bow with the other cast, the applause, the sense of accomplishment, the privilege of serving my church and community and the friendship of the people bowing with me, all combined into one of the most amazing feelings of exhilaration that I have ever felt.

That brief but powerful moment of exhilaration was built on hours of effort, vulnerability, stress, sweat and physical pain (dancing requires fitness and flexibility, and I possess neither!!) But what I was doing aligned with my values and passions, which made it all worthwhile.

My Christmas performance is a metaphor for our lives with ACT. Life is full of hard work and discomfort. Unpleasant feelings are going to happen anyway. We might as well experience them in pursuit of our values, rather than simply spend all of our time trying to avoid them.

Principles of ACT

ACT does this through six principles. The first three relate to effectively handling painful thoughts and feelings, and the second three help create a rich and fulfilling life. These are:

1. DEFUSION–relating to your thoughts in a new way. Rather than fighting them or trying to suppress them, defusion involves learning to see thoughts for what they really are ... just words, without real power.

2. EXPANSION–making room for unpleasant feelings instead of fighting them or trying to suppress them. It involves accepting them for what they are and giving them space so they become less bothersome.

3. CONNECTION–living in the present and being fully engaged with what's in the here-and-now, rather than dwelling on the past or stressing about the future.

4. THE OBSERVING SELF–Learning to take a different mental perspective and simply observe our inner thoughts and feelings.

5. VALUES–Understanding what our values truly are, that is, what's significant and meaningful to us as a person.

6. COMMITTED ACTION–Taking effective action based on our values, action that's committed (that is, action we will take over and over again, no matter how many times we fail or go off track.)

FACT

As a spiritually neutral psychological therapy, ACT has seen amazing improvements in a wide range of psychiatric illnesses, and has contributed to the improved life satisfaction of people all over the world, of all different religions.[69-73] As I said before, ACT is not a specifically Christian technique, and it was developed outside of a Biblical context.

Though the same principles from ACT are found woven through the Bible. When the Biblical principles are brought together in to the ACT framework, the power of the Bible's teaching over the centuries starts to make sense. In this context, we have a powerful psychological therapy combined with the truth of the Bible, something that can exponentially grow our lives as Christians. I call this 'FACT'.

FACT is simply Faith-based Acceptance and Commitment Therapy. It's the principles of ACT brought together by a common value to all Christians—our love for God—and understood in the context of the corresponding Biblical principles. I'm not going to make outlandish claims that FACT is better than ACT, but the benefit to the average Christian in FACT is simply that it connects a number of Biblical principles that are often taught individually, and it encourages effective action towards our common goal of knowing God based on the common value inherent to the Christian life, which is our faith and love of God.

Principles of FACT

1. Defusion

As Christians, we have the same concerns that are common to all of human kind, like wanting to be accepted, wanting to be healthy, wanting to be safe. But we can also be vulnerable to a number of other thoughts that are specific to our lives as Christians, thoughts that hinder us from accepting God's forgiveness or from coming into his presence.

Thoughts like:
"I'm not worthy."
"God doesn't really love me."
"My sin keeps me from God's presence."
"I don't try hard enough."
"I don't pray enough."
"My faith isn't strong enough."

These aren't the only ones. Everyone will have their own particular thoughts that they struggle with when it comes to living out our Christian faith in full. What's yours? Feel free to even put the book down for a moment and think about it, or bring it to God in prayer. Write it down somewhere when that recurrent thought comes to mind.

Those thoughts can be very distressing, but they're normal. Remember, our brain is a "don't get killed" organ. It constantly looks for danger and deficiency so we can avoid injury and banishment. If we didn't have those thoughts, we'd be roadkill or lunch for some large animal, or we wouldn't remain as part of our social group, something which provides safety in numbers.

Defusion involves simply recognising those thoughts for what they are ... just thoughts. They're just words on a screen inside your mind. Some of them may be right (you really may not pray enough) or they may be our normal danger-discerning part of our brain taking over in the faith-part of our lives.

Dealing with those thoughts involves some acceptance and thankfulness. We'll talk more about this later, but a simple exercise to try when you recognise that recurrent thought is simply to acknowledge it, "I notice that I'm having the thought that..." Then quietly say or think to yourself, "Thanks God".

So, for example, "I notice that I'm having the thought that I don't pray enough. Thanks God."

It may seem strange at first, but give it a try.

Also, just to clarify that we're not thanking God for the fact we don't pray enough, we're accepting and thanking God that our brains are doing what they're built for – our "don't get killed" organ is doing its job. Use the thoughts that are true and helpful. If they're not true and not helpful, you can let them go. After all, they're just words. But fundamentally, accept them without judgement.

2. *Expansion*

Sometimes we have feelings that are much the same as those recurrent thoughts. We can feel low. We can feel inadequate. We can feel apathetic. Sometimes we can feel angry. Having feelings is normal; this is the way God made us. Jesus experienced and acted on his feelings. He was happy, he was hungry, he was tired, he was sad, he grieved, and he was angry. There's nothing wrong with having feelings, but they can be problematic when they take our focus away from those things that are important.

Fighting with your emotions is the wrong way to handle them. We need to practice expansion instead, literally making room for those feelings. Usually if we experience a feeling we don't like, we tend to tighten up, trying to resist them. Instead, we need to be able to give those feelings room so that they don't constrict us. The feelings are still there, and you don't have to like the feelings being there, but expansion means that you don't have to spend all your energy fighting them, devoting your energy to that which is valuable to you instead.

Like defusion, expansion simply involves acknowledging the feeling, and expressing gratitude. You can give that feeling a name, or describe it.

Then take a full breath in, slowly out, and say or think to yourself, "I notice that I'm having the feeling ..." and say "Thanks God".

So, for example, "I notice that I'm having the angry feeling. Thanks God."

Again, it seems strange at first. Our natural human response is to resist or to fight, but this usually makes the feelings worse. Giving the feelings more room will help to reframe the feelings as just that, simply feelings that we have naturally every day in the marvellous bodies that God created for us. So let them be, and thank God for them.

3. Connection

Connection in the ACT framework is about the experience of the present moment. It looks at what's going on in the here-and-now without getting excessively caught up in the past (which you can't change) and the future (which is unpredictable).

The Biblical correlation here is also thankfulness. 1 Thessalonians 5:18 says, "In every thing give thanks: for this is the will of God in Christ Jesus concerning you." Thanking God for what you have in the here and now brings you back to the present moment, away from the if-only's of the past and the what-if's of the future.

I think Philippians 4:6 sums it up well, "Be anxious for nothing; but in every thing by prayer and supplication with thanksgiving let your requests be made known unto God."

4. The Observing Self

Ok, so there's no verse in the Bible that says, "Thou shalt observe thine self."

Even though there's no direct correlation of this principle in the Bible, there is a number of examples of great men of the Bible using the principle of the observing self. King David offers the best example. So often in the psalms that he authored, he talks to a part of himself, which he addresses as his 'soul'. For example, in Psalm 42:5, "Why, my soul, are you downcast? Why so disturbed within me? Put your hope in God, for I will yet praise him, my Saviour and my God." King David is standing on the outside of his soul, his emotional, feeling self and looking in. He's using the principle of the observing self.

The example of King David shows that the principle of the Observing Self is a good one to utilise for daily prayer and meditation on the Bible, because it helps us to learn what our normal thoughts and feelings are, which may enhance our discernment of the still small voice of the Holy Spirit from the constant inner chatter of our normal mind.

5. Values

In ACT, values refer to those core principles that guide us and motivate us. Values provide purpose. All people have values, but as Christians, we believe our values stem from our God-given purpose and abilities.

In Ephesians 2:10, Paul wrote, "For we are God's workmanship, created in Christ Jesus to do good works, which God prepared in advance for us to do."

This is a very powerful verse! So is the passage of scripture that it's nested in. Take the time to read the whole of Ephesians 2 when you have a moment.

If something was created for a purpose, then the very act of creation was purposeful. If I were to make a knife, I would have to shape it specifically with the correct dimensions, make it pointed, make it sharp.

I can't just pour some molten metal on the floor and hope it comes out straight or sharp.

In the same way, God designed us specifically for certain tasks. He didn't just throw a few limbs and some skin together and hope for the best. Our life is not a conglomeration of random chance. Whatever your purpose in life, you're meant to be who you are.

If we dig a little deeper into the original Greek language, the meaning of the verse becomes even clearer. 'Workmanship' in the Greek is *poiema* from which we get our English word 'poem'. We're not a meaningless jumble of letters that make no sense; we are a beautifully crafted blend of rhythm, harmony and meaning. You're a sonnet from the mouth of God.

Following in this vein, the next word 'created' is the word *ktizo* which refers to God creating the worlds, or to form or shape, literally "to transform completely." Like a potter taking a lump of clay and completely transforming it into a ceramic vase, when God spoke you into being, you were expertly crafted into the symphony of shape, colour, texture and depth that makes you unique.

Our values reflect the unique gifts and abilities that God has created in each one of us, and when we learn to tap into our values, we unlock the vast potential energy of purpose which then drives committed action.

6. Committed Action

According to the ACT framework, the last principle that leads to a meaningful life is committed action, which is action that's effective, and that you take again and again no matter how many times you drift away from it. Committed action is shorthand for "committed, effective, valued action."[74]

This is akin to the Christian principle of faith. "Now faith is the substance of things hoped for, the evidence of things not seen." (Hebrews 11:1) Those things hoped for and not seen are our values – our love for God, our belief in the power of God, our belief in our eternal destiny. Faith is the outward working of those hopes, the evidence of them. This is done through action: "Faith without works is dead." (James 2).

For example, if we value fellowship, one expression of committed action is by attending church regularly even if the music isn't our favourite style, or the people are cliquey or catty. If our value is understanding God's word, then one expression of committed action would be to read the Bible every day, or to listen to expository podcasts, or to enrol in some subjects in Biblical Greek through a local Bible College or seminary.

Values often guide our "ministry" within the church as well as how we express or live out our Christian lives. It's almost a given that as Christians, our love for God is one of our values, which means that even though we will inevitably fail God, committed action will bring us back to reading the Bible and praying, and serving him, in spite of the guilt and condemnation that we naturally experience because we failed.

The journey of faith

Just one more thing about values and committed action... in the ACT literature, values are often equated to a direction, like west. Technically "west" is infinite. There are places along the journey west, and these places are finite, but there is always further west that you can travel.

For example, if I travel west from my home in Brisbane, I will eventually get to Perth on the other side of Australia. Perth is a finite distance, a place on the journey, but I can keep travelling west from Perth. Eventually I'd hit Africa, then another long swim to South America. If I kept going, I would make it back to Australia, but I could still keep going west if I wanted to.

Our Christian journey is the same ... not that we keep going around in circles, although I know it feels like that sometimes. Rather, there is always further to go. Even the Apostle Paul, one of the strongest Christians in recorded history, said this, "Not that I have already attained, or am already perfected; but I press on, that I may lay hold of that for which Christ Jesus has also laid hold of me. Brethren, I do not count myself to have apprehended; but one thing I do, forgetting those things which are behind and reaching forward to those things which are ahead, I press toward the goal for the prize of the upward call of God in Christ Jesus." Philippians 3:12-14

This passage was the inspiration for my high school's motto, "I press towards the goal." Having it forced upon me for several years as a rebellious adolescent made me somewhat indifferent to this very powerful scripture, but as I've come to understand the power of values and committed action, I've developed a much deeper appreciation of Paul's words.

Not even the Apostle Paul, the guy who had visions of heaven and wrote most of the New Testament, felt like he had reached the end of his values journey. When he wrote, "I press towards the goal," he demonstrated the power of values and committed action that we can apply to our lives as we travel on our own individual faith journeys.

Summary

FACT is the fusion of the principles of the Bible with the framework of Acceptance and Commitment Therapy. ACT is about creating a rich and meaningful life, while accepting the discomfort that inevitably goes with it. It involves taking effective action guided by our deepest values and in which we are fully present and engaged. In ACT, we recognise that we don't have to fight with our thoughts and feelings, but that we can live in the present moment, being guided by our deepest values.

All Christians share common values: our love for God and our commitment to the gospel of Jesus Christ. And the principles of the Bible support the framework of ACT. By focusing on God and exercising gratitude, and through committed faith action, we can live the rich and fulfilling life that God promises to those who love Him.

We'll come back to ACT and FACT in future chapters, but we can also use these principles to maintain good mental health, which we'll discuss in the next chapter.

7

Ingredients for Good Mental Health

Life shouldn't just be about avoiding poor health, but also enjoying good health. Our psychological health is no different.

Before we take a look at poor mental health, let's look at some of the ways that people can enjoy good mental health and wellbeing. This chapter will discuss seven elements that are Biblically and scientifically recognised as keys to help people living richer and more fulfilling lives.

These aren't the only ways that a person can find fulfilment. They're not sure-fire ways of preventing all mental health problems. They're not seven steps to enlightenment or happiness. But applying these principles can improve psychosocial wellbeing, and encourage good mental health.

1. *Temet nosce*—"Know thyself"

Generally speaking, there are two ways that a person can live their lives, as a boat or as a buoy—those who set out to find life or to let life find them.

Some people are quite content to be buoys—to stay in the same place and let the social currents and tides bring things to them. They're more passive in their approach, content to accept that life will come and go as it pleases. Then there are the boats, those who don't want to stay in the one place, but want to chart their own course and discover life for themselves.

By the way, it's not that being a boat is better than being a buoy, or vice versa. You are who you are. Boats need buoys, and buoys need boats. If you're a buoy, you're strong and stable. You can help boats know where they can safely sail.

For those people who're boats, who want to sail their own course and discover life, it helps a lot in the journey to know where you're going.

This may seem obvious enough. In fact, it seems too obvious—we often think we know where we're going when in reality, we haven't a clue where we really want to go or how to get there.

The first question is, "Where do you *want* to go?" Some of us are gifted with an amazing confidence, self-assurance and motivation, and have the ten-year plan all mapped out, but those people are the minority. It's fine if we don't know where exactly we want to go, but at the very least, we should know the direction we wish to sail in, which is guided by our values.

As we discussed in the last chapter, 'values' can mean different things to different people, but in the Acceptance and Commitment framework, values refer to "Leading principles that can guide us and motivate us as we move through life", "Our heart's deepest desires: how we want to be, what we want to stand for and how we want to relate to the world around us." [74]

Values help define us, and living by our values is an ongoing process that never really reaches an end. Living according to your values is like sailing due west. No matter how far you travel, there is always further west you can go. While travelling west, there will be stops along the way, stopovers along our direction of travel like islands or reefs. These are like our goals in life.

The difference between goals and values is important. You could set yourself a whole list of different goals, and achieve every one of them, but not necessarily find meaning or fulfilment if they all go against the underlying values that you have. So goals are empty and unfulfilling if they aren't undergirded by your deeper values.

How can you understand your values? There are a couple of ways. Ask yourself: "What do I find myself really passionate about? What things irk me? If I could do anything I wanted, and money was no object, what would I do?" Is there a recurrent theme running through your answers?

I've always found myself irritated by misleading mass-marketing, and more recently by disingenuous social media memes and unscientific health messages. The common theme ... 'truth'. I know, it sounds a bit trite, like some second-rate comic book hero, but I've mulled this over a lot, and for me, 'truth' is one of my deepest values.

There are other ways to discover what your values are. Some people have suggested writing your own eulogy (the speech someone gives about you at your funeral). It sounds a bit morbid, and it's only a figurative exercise, but it tends to sharply clarify what you want your life to be like. What do you want your legacy to be? Think about the things that you want to be known for at the end of your life, and see if there's a word that best describes those desires.

If that's a bit too confronting, there are some on-line tools that can also give you an idea. There is only so much a long list of questions can discover about you, but results of these surveys can provide a starting point for further thought. There are a couple of free resources that may be helpful (though you will have to register): * https://www.authentichappiness.sas.upenn.edu–and click on the dropdownmenuinthe "Questionnaires" section, andselect "Brief strengthstest"

* http://www.viacharacter.org/Survey/Account/Register

One final note on the buoys and the boats—whether you're a buoy or a boat, you're still going to encounter large waves, strong currents and wild storms, as well as peaceful weather. As a buoy, those adverse conditions will simply find you where you are. You can't escape from them. You're also going to experience those same large waves, strong currents and wild storms as a boat. The difference is that buoys have no choice but to ride out the adverse conditions. Boats, on the other hand, can use the energy of the difficult circumstances to power them to their destinations, so long as they harness them correctly.

Boats can't outrun bad weather all the time. Adversity is inevitable. Happiness, contentment, enlightenment, or whatever you're seeking, isn't found in avoiding or controlling your adverse circumstances, but in learning how to follow your values in the midst of the calm weather or the storm.

As I discussed in the last chapter, as Christians, one of our common values is our love for God and our desire to follow Jesus. Scripture teaches that each of us has our own unique path to follow. Ephesians 2:10, "For we are God's workmanship, created in Christ Jesus to do good works, which God prepared in advance for us to do." Remember, we're a beautifully crafted blend of rhythm, harmony and meaning, a sonnet from the mouth of God. I believe that our individual purpose stems from our common purpose and values, like leaves are dependant on the branches, trunk and roots of the tree. I heard a brilliant summary of the purpose of the Christian life, which was simply "To know Christ, and to make Christ known." I believe that it's this common value, shared by all Christians, from which our direction in life stems.

In knowing our values, we can know ourselves, and engage in life in its fullness.

2. Be kind

One of the best things you can do for your health and happiness is to be kind to other people. Altruism activates rewarding neural networks, essentially the same brain regions as those activated when receiving rewards or experiencing pleasure. Studies also show that both the hormones and the neurotransmitters in the brain involved in helping behaviour and social bonding can lessen stress levels and anxiety. The immune system and autonomic nervous systems are positively affected by the quality and extent of social networks, and increased sociability and concern for others' wellbeing can improve immune system and stress responses.[75]

The Bible has always encouraged us to show other people kindness. In Ephesians 4:31-32, Paul tells the church at Ephesus, "Get rid of all bitterness, rage and anger, brawling and slander, along with every form of malice. Be kind and compassionate to one another, forgiving each other, just as in Christ God forgave you." And that kindness wasn't just for other people in the church, but to anyone in need (Matthew 25:34-40).

There are infinite ways to show kindness, but the thing that links them together is unselfishness, the "disinterested and selfless concern for the well-being of others", or in less formal language, simply giving with no strings attached.

If you're looking for some ideas on some new ways to show kindness, the Random Acts of Kindness Foundation has plenty of them.

Check out https://www.randomactsofkindness.org/kindness-ideas

3. Mindfulness

Mindfulness is a practice that we can all become better at.

Mindfulness involves paying attention to things in the present moment, and away from those thoughts that drag us into the faults of the past or the fear of the future.[74] While there are a number of ways in which mindfulness is considered in psychology and different religions, I consider mindfulness simply as non-judgemental awareness of one's moment-to-moment experience, which is also how it's considered in the ACT framework.

In other words, when we're mindful, we experience our internal and external realities and accept them for what they are, not judge them as good or bad or positive or negative. We fully accept our experience of events, without becoming excessively preoccupied with the experience or trying to suppress the experience.

People who are naturally mindful are more likely to have higher levels of life satisfaction, agreeableness, conscientiousness, vitality, self esteem, empathy, sense of autonomy, competence, optimism, and pleasant affect, and are less likely to have depression, neuroticism, absent-mindedness, dissociation, rumination, cognitive reactivity, social anxiety, difficulties in emotion regulation, experiential avoidance and general psychological symptoms.

So mindfulness is certainly a good trait to have, although it needs to be said that all of these positive traits are currently just an association of mindfulness. That is, people who are mindful have higher levels of life satisfaction *et cetera*, but we don't know if mindfulness causes higher levels of life satisfaction *et cetera*. Though it's also interesting to note some more recent research into mindfulness that shows that people who are not naturally mindful, but who are taught to practice mindfulness skills, also demonstrate an increased ability to cope with habitual urges (like a desire to smoke, for example), feelings of anxiety, low mood, and fearfulness.[76]

Mindfulness has some overlap with the psychological skill of acceptance. In mindfulness, we not only stop fighting with our feelings and thoughts, but we take a step back to pay attention to them and observe them in a non-judgemental way. With acceptance, we acknowledge the thoughts and feelings, but divert our attention to other things.

To clarify, mindfulness is non-judgementally observing our thoughts, feelings and emotions, not fighting with them to suppress them, or passively allowing our thoughts and feelings to overwhelm us. If our thoughts or feelings were like a hungry lion, mindfulness is standing outside of the lion enclosure, observing the different characteristics of the lion, rather than jumping into the enclosure to try and subdue it, or passively standing in the enclosure waiting to become lunch.

Mindfulness doesn't need special training. Being mindful is simply being aware of your thoughts, feelings and emotions, and accepting them for what they are:

- How are you feeling at the moment?

- What are you feeling at the moment? (Are you happy at the moment, or anxious, or restless etc.?)

- What does that feel like in your body?

- Where is that feeling in your body?

- Describe the feeling ... hot or cold, squeezing, searing, heavy or light?

- Do you have an urge to do something, like have some chocolate or smoke a cigarette?

- What's that urge like?

- Can you put it into words?

Only one word of warning: It would be fair to assume that someone will be reading this book who's experienced some severe trauma in their lives. Both acceptance and mindfulness will help to manage the feelings that your trauma will inevitably cause. If the severity of that trauma causes you to be overwhelmed by your feelings, however, I encourage you to still tackle those memories and emotions using mindfulness, but don't feel like you have to do it on your own. Work with a psychologist or doctor who is experienced in mindfulness-based therapies, so there is someone to assist you through the process until you get better and stronger, so you're not overwhelmed.

Often mindfulness is taught as a contemplative activity, that is, we think about the feelings as we observe them. There is nothing wrong, however, with expressing your mindfulness in other ways, like drawing, painting or movement. You can express how you're feeling in writing, or through a journal. I often read through the Psalms that King David wrote, and wonder if he was modelling mindfulness for us in the way he acknowledged and described his feelings in the words that he wrote as prayer and poetry. Find what works best for you as you grow in the skill of mindfulness.

4. Show some SSAS

SSAS stands for Supple, Strong And Skilful. This applies physically and mentally.

Physical fitness is good for us. This isn't the main point of the chapter, but I've never seen a study that shows exercise to be a bad thing. Ultimately, it's not how fat you are that's important for your longevity, it's how fit you are.[77, 78] And the way to get fit is to exercise.

Physical exercise isn't just good for the body but good for the brain as well. While the exact pathways are still being determined, there's good evidence that moderate regular physical activity improves the balance of pro- and anti-inflammatory mediators in the body and in the brain. In the brain, this improves the overall function of our brain cells and their ability to form new pathways, which in turn, has been shown to improve mood disorders like anxiety and depression.[79]

Being SSAS isn't just about what being physically fit and active can do for your mood, but it also relates to being psychologically flexible and using psychological skills to leverage your strengths rather than just fighting with your weaknesses. One of the keys here is acceptance. Using your values that we spoke about earlier as your guide, exploit the things that you're good at, using them to gain some self-confidence and momentum. Accept the things that can't be changed in your life. Then when you have some momentum, learn some new skills to increase your resilience and strengthen your weaknesses.

I say this because sometimes we spend so much time focussing on all the bad things in our lives that we forget about the good things that we already have or can already do. It would be like an athlete spending all their time in the gym, getting really fit and strong, but never getting onto the field or court. It's important that we courageously challenge ourselves to turn our weak points into strong points, but it's more important to do what we can to help others around us.

5. Be grateful

As I was meandering through Facebook one day, I came across this post by Sir Richard Branson, founder of Virgin: "Thanked an airport security worker, he said I was the first to say #ThankYou in three years. Shocked! Saying thank you should be second nature ..."

Richard Branson #ThankYou

Perhaps the security worker was exaggerating for the billionaire, or perhaps everybody hates airport security at the airport where he works. At any rate, three years is a long time to go without someone saying thanks.

As Sir Richard said, "Saying thank you should be second nature..." Saying thanks is a small part of the much larger psychology of gratitude, which is "part of a wider life orientation towards noticing and appreciating the positive in the world."[80]

In fact, there are several components to the overall orientation of gratitude, including:

1. individual differences in the experience of grateful affect,

2. appreciation of other people,

3. a focus on what the person has,

4. feelings of awe when encountering beauty,

5. behaviours to express gratitude,

6. appreciation rising from understanding that life is short,

7. a focus on the positive in the present moment, and

8. positive social comparisons.[80]

The research suggests that people who are naturally grateful tend to be less angry and hostile, less depressed, less emotionally vulnerable, and experienced positive emotions more frequently. Gratitude also correlates with traits like positive social functioning, emotional warmth, gregariousness, activity seeking, trust, altruism, and tender-mindedness. Grateful people also had higher openness to their feeling, ideas, and values, and greater competence, dutifulness, and achievement striving.

Like mindfulness, these effects may be simply an association of gratitude with other personality traits. In other words, people who are naturally optimistic or conscientious are also more likely to be thankful, rather than the thankfulness causing someone to be more optimistic or conscientious. There are a few studies that show that gratitude interventions improve self-worth, body image, and anxiety, although the evidence is that while gratitude was better than doing nothing, it was equal to, not superior to, currently accepted psychological interventions.

Even though gratitude may not be better than standard psychological treatments, it's better than doing nothing and it's easy to do. The best studied gratitude intervention is a gratitude diary – writing something down every day that you're thankful for.[80] It doesn't have to be long. A single sentence or phrase is good enough. It doesn't even have to be written, if that's not your thing. I had a friend who was determined to do a gratitude journal, but she also had a love of and a knack for photography. So, she decided to take a photo a day of something that she was grateful for, and then post it on Facebook. She had her moments when she doubted herself, when she struggled to find a subject of her gratitude, or struggled to find something unique (especially after day 300), but the end result was amazing. She grew in her gratitude and her photographic skill, and I often found myself blessed by her beautiful images and insights.

So, be thankful and express it in your own unique way.

6. Forgiveness

"You'd think after five months of lying on my back, I would have given up any idea of getting even, just be a nice guy and call it a day. Nice guys are fine: you have to have somebody to take advantage of... but they always finish last."

Mel Gibson's character spoke these words as an introduction to the movie "Payback." The plotline of the movie sees him maim or kill every person linked in the chain of thugs and organised crime that ripped him off of his seventy thousand dollars. At the end of the movie, after he exacts the final revenge on the last villain, he drives off with his money and his renewed romance. His vengeance was fulfilled. The directors of the movie implied that he was happy. But if that was real life, would he have been happy, or would he have just been even?

It's human nature to repay wrong with another wrong. Eye for an eye, tooth for a tooth. If you hurt me, natural justice is fulfilled if I make you feel the same pain in return. So what choices do you have if someone hurts or wrongs you? Well, you could retaliate. You could plan retribution. Ask for recompense. Or simply push for recognition of your pain. Sometimes these strategies lead to resolution, but usually not immediately, and in order to stay motivated to achieve a delayed resolution, you have to keep reminding yourself of the pain caused to you, so that the effort you're making will be worthwhile.

As the old proverb goes, "Two wrongs don't make a right." If you hurt me, hurting you back doesn't make my pain go away. It just adds more pain to the world, because I'm still in pain and now you're in pain. Then you'll want to hurt me back, and the cycle escalates. Francis Bacon said, "A man that studieth revenge keeps his own wounds green, which otherwise would heal and do well." In other words, you may be able to bring about retribution, but during the process, you'll end up keeping your own wounds open and festering, instead of letting them close and heal. It's like someone cut you with a knife, and in order to show them what damage they did to you, you keep reopening the wound every few days. The wound may look open and fresh should they ever care to notice, but you're the one who had to put up with an open wound for an extended time, and re-live the pain every time you reopened it.

Interestingly, research tends to support this notion. One study showed that when subjects were asked to think of reacting aggressively to a given scenario, parts of the limbic system in their brains increased in activity. This isn't unsurprising, given that our brain subconsciously prepares us all the time for fight or flight responses when it starts to sense danger, in preparation for possible action.

What was more interesting is that angry rumination also reduced the activity of the subject's frontal lobes as well, which is really important for reasoning. So it might be that reasoning is disrupted by anger, and that rehearsing angry and aggressive mental scenarios shuts down the brains problem solving approach and calm emotions.[81]

The other alternative to nursing the grudge is forgiveness. Forgiveness is a particular form of acceptance. It's the act of moving on from insult or injustice. It isn't saying that what was done to you was ok, but rather, that you aren't going to be held captive by it.

Forgiveness is actually a complex psychological process. There have been lots of studies looking at different aspects of forgiveness, but without getting bogged down in details, forgiveness helps to rebalance things. People who forgive habitually tend to also have lower blood pressure, while individual acts of forgiveness and lower hostility predict lower stress levels, which in turn predicts lower self-reported illness. The reduction of negative affect (a "bad mood") was the strongest mediator between forgiveness and physical health symptoms, although the study authors noted other variables such as spirituality, social skills, and lower stress also had a role in the forgiveness-health relationship.[82]

I understand that talking about forgiveness can bring up some deep and difficult feelings in some people. Just like physical wounds, some traumas are shallow and heal quickly, but others are inflicted so deep that they are hard to heal, like rape, childhood abuse, domestic violence and other deep psychological insults. It's important to clarify here that memories of such traumatic events often intrude into your conscious awareness, where it takes over and replays in your memory. That's different to unforgiveness and rumination, which are memories that we foster and encourage by actively rehearsing them. Forgiveness is still a part of the healing process of severe psychological trauma, but the healing process may take longer, and the process of finding that forgiveness may require a professional to help walk through the process. If you've been the victim of a severe trauma, you don't need to go it alone. Find a psychologist or talk to your doctor if you're not sure.

For the Christian, forgiveness is at the very core of the entire life of faith we lead. God forgave us, and we can enjoy that forgiveness if we choose to move away from a life enslaved to sin. It's through the death of Jesus on the cross that we have this chance, and Jesus himself demonstrated the ultimate forgiveness when, as he hung dying on the cross, he forgave the soldiers that put him there. Throughout his ministry, he preached the same message. Forgiveness is a central text of the Lord's prayer, he told Peter that he should forgive someone "seventy times seven", and he showed grace to those around him such as the woman caught in adultery. There are many more examples of forgiveness in the Bible as well.

I don't know if there is any one particular method to forgive. Apologies help,[83] but they aren't necessary to be able to forgive someone. Sometimes people find actually saying the words "I forgive you" to be a powerful release. That can be to a person directly, although that may not always go down so well. Saying it internally is valid. Sometimes writing it in a letter, and then tearing it up as an act of finality, can be useful.

Find what works for you. I hope that you can find it in your heart to forgive those in your life that have wronged you and continue to move forward. Remember, "To forgive is to set a prisoner free, and discover that the prisoner was you." (Lewis B. Smedes)

7. Create social networks

Before 2004, everyone knew what social networks were. Now when you talk about 'social networks', people assume you're referring to Facebook. It seems like virtual social networking has been around forever, but real social networking in communities has been around a lot longer.

We know this because we're wired for social interaction, with specific areas of the brain devoted to social behaviour, such as the orbitofrontal cortex. There are also neurotransmitters and hormones that are strongly associated with bonding and maintenance of social relationships, like oxytocin and β-endorphins. Research has shown that both humans and other primates find social stimuli intrinsically rewarding—babies look longer at faces than at non-face stimuli, for example.[84]

People who engage in social relationships are more likely to live longer, some estimate by an extra 50%.[85] We also know that the opposite is true. Loneliness predicts depressive symptoms, impaired sleep and daytime dysfunction, reductions in physical activity, and impaired mental health and cognition. At the biological level, loneliness is associated with altered blood pressure, increased stress hormone secretion, a shift in the balance of cytokines towards inflammation and altered immunity. Loneliness may predict a shortened life-span.[86]

It's important to understand what loneliness is, and conversely, what defines good social relationships? Fundamentally, good or bad social relationships are related to the *quality* of the social interaction. This rule applies equally to real social networks[86] and their on-line equivalents.[87] So quality is fundamentally more important than quantity in terms of friendships, with that quality strongly determined by the connection within those social relationships. For example, loneliness "can be thought of as perceived isolation and is more accurately defined as the distressing feeling that accompanies discrepancies between one's desired and actual social relationships."[86]

The corollary is that friendship can be thought of as perceived connection within social relationships, or the comforting feeling that accompanies the match between one's desired and actual social relationships.

So healthy social relationships aren't defined by the size of your network, but by the strength of the connections that your network contains, relative to what's important to you. Just because you're not a vivacious extrovert who is friends with everyone doesn't mean that your social network is lacking. It also means that you can have meaningful connections to friends through social media, just as much as you can have meaningful connections through face-to-face interactions. It's not the way you interact, but the quality of the connection that counts.

What is it about other people that makes us more likely to be their friends? Connection between friends is often the result of attraction to individuals of similar personalities or skills, although recent research suggests that friendship may be influenced by factors on a genetic level. For example, one set of research suggests that unrelated friends are more likely to be genetically similar, equivalent to the level of fourth cousins, compared to unrelated strangers.[84]

As Christians, we're encouraged to engage with other Christians on a regular basis, which in our modern world, is through regular church attendance. As the Bible says in Hebrews 10:23-25, "Let us hold unswervingly to the hope we profess, for he who promised is faithful. And let us consider how we may spur one another on towards love and good deeds, not giving up meeting together, as some are in the habit of doing, but encouraging one another – and all the more as you see the Day approaching."

As the research has shown, it's not just being part of the crowd, but connecting with those in the church in a meaningful way. It's very easy to be lonely in a crowded church.

Always remember the golden rule: "Befriend, and be a friend." That's how you'll find benefit to your spirit, soul and body.

Summary

In this chapter, we've looked at things that we can all do to help us live at optimal mental health. If only it was always as easy as just following the seven steps. Sometimes we can do all the right things and still find ourselves struggling with poor mental health.

In the next part of the book, we're going to review some of the most common forms of mental ill health, what they're caused by, and how, as Christians, we can manage them best.

8

Stress, Resilience and the Tap Model

Hans Selye, a pioneer in stress research, said once that, "Everybody knows what stress is, but no one really knows."[88]

We may not know exactly what it is, but we know how to grumble about it. As Robert A. Shweder wrote once in the New York Times, "'I'm stressed out' is non-accusatory, apolitical and detached. It is a good way to keep the peace and, at the same time, a low-cost way to complain."[89]

The term stress generally refers to "experiences that cause feelings of anxiety and frustration because they push us beyond our ability to successfully cope"[90] though scientifically, stress has been difficult to pin down. Different researchers often use different definitions of stress depending on what they're studying or what field of psychology or science they belong to.[91]

This chapter is an introduction to the concepts of stress and coping. The balance of stress and coping is an integral part of what constitutes good (or bad) mental health for each person, and we will talk about these concepts again when we discuss common mental illnesses later in the book.

A broad concept of stress

To gain a better understanding of stress, it's useful to step away from the medical concept of stress, and think about what the term means in other fields.

When an engineer thinks about stress, it's usually in relation to a physical force on a material object. There was an episode of Mythbusters where they tested the myth of Pykrete, a material that was nothing but wood shavings and ice. They were testing to see whether it was stronger than ice alone, whether it was bulletproof, and whether it could be used to build a boat![92] The Mythbusters made some in their workshop and tested it to compare its strength with normal ice.

How did they test it? By *stressing* it–placing weights on the end of the block of the ice/pykrete until it broke. (In the end, pykrete was ten times stronger than ice, was bulletproof, and they made a fully operational motor-boat from it!)

So the mechanical definition of stress is, "pressure or tension exerted on a material object."[15] There are a few illustrations of mechanical stress, in our bodies and in everyday life, that are good metaphors for stress in our lives.

The Classical Stress/Productivity Curve

I really don't know a lot about guitars, but I do know that when you first put a new string on the guitar, it's unstretched – there's no strain on it at all. If all you did was tied the two ends of the string to the tone peg and the tuning peg, the string would remain limp and lifeless. It wouldn't be able to do anything useful. It certainly wouldn't play a note.

When the tuning peg is twisted a few times, there is some tightness in the wire. The string is now under tension (i.e. stress). It's now able to play a note of some form, so it can do some work and fulfil some of the function of a guitar string, though the note's out of tune.

With a small adjustment, the string reaches its optimal tension and can play the correct note! This is the point where the string is fulfilling its designed purpose. Optimal stress equals optimal function.

With further tightening of the string, the perfect pitch is lost, but the string can still produce a sound of some form. With more tension, the string can still make a noise, but it's off-pitch, and on a microscopic level, the fibres inside the cord are starting to tear. If the string were wound further and further, it would eventually break.

If this ratio of the tension of the string versus the usefulness of the string were to be plotted as a graph, it would look like an upside down "U". This is the classic stress/productivity curve.

The stress/productivity curve has two special points, the Point of Maximum Productivity, and the Point of Maximum Growth. For now, remember the names. I'll explain more about them soon.

The Stress-Productivity Curve

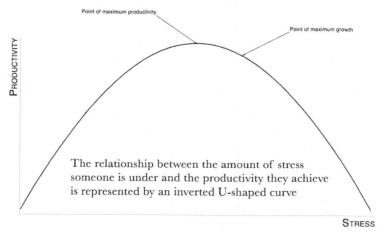

Point of maximum productivity

Point of maximum growth

PRODUCTIVITY

The relationship between the amount of stress someone is under and the productivity they achieve is represented by an inverted U-shaped curve

STRESS

The Exponential Stress/Productivity Curve

The second metaphor that I think illustrates a different concept of the stress/productivity relationship is a car.

I really don't know a lot about cars either. I know the important things like where the petrol goes, and how to drive them, but otherwise cars are very mysterious and powerful devices, their mystery is only exceeded by their power.

What I do know is that the engine is very much like the guitar string. As more petrol is fed into the engine, the engine gets more powerful. Soon, the engine finds its "power band", a zone of maximum torque that can be achieved at moderate revolutions. As the engine is given more gas, the power output declines from the middle of the power band. If the engine was maxed out, then the amount of functional power coming out is reduced.

This would plot as a similar graph to the U-curve of the stress/productivity curve. But cars not only have engines, but also a gearbox. The gears allow for multiplication of the work done (the productivity) for the same stress on the engine.

G-Force!

As a child, I didn't dream of becoming an astronaut, but I was interested in space. The beauty of our night sky is as stunning as any forest, river or mountain. I would read of the astronauts in rockets and in space stations, floating around in zero gravity, swimming through the "air". That sounded like a lot of fun.

But zero gravity isn't particularly good for you. Some early astronauts had to be carried off their landing craft on stretchers because the effect of zero gravity would render these men weak and atrophied. They boarded the spacecraft at the peak of their physical strength and fitness, but after only a few weeks without gravity, their bodies resembled that of the elderly (although without the wrinkles).[93]

It's a general principle of the human body that any tissue that isn't used shrinks in size – a process called atrophy. In zero gravity, the body doesn't need as much muscle, so the muscles shrink. The body doesn't need as much bone strength, so the bones weaken. There is no gravity to pull their blood away from their head, so the blood volume decreases. Because there's less muscle to pump blood to, and less blood to pump, the heart doesn't work as hard, so the heart muscle atrophies. The net effect of zero gravity is to make you physically weak.[93]

On the other hand, too much gravity is not great either. Animals can adapt to small amounts of hypergravity,[94] but large amounts aren't so good. During astronaut training, NASA subjects the rookie spacemen to rigorous tests including placing them in a large centrifuge and spinning it very fast. The result is an increase in the gravitational forces applied to their bodies. The increased gravity makes everything in the body heavier and their blood is pulled towards the legs and away from the brain, which leads to what is known as G-LOC (Gravity-induced Loss Of Consciousness). In other words, the heart can't fight the increased force of gravity and the brain loses its blood supply, which makes you pass out. Josh McHugh did an entertaining piece on his experience with G-LOC and the centrifuge in Wired (2003).[95]

In this sense, gravity is to us physically like stress is to us mentally. Without gravity, our physical bodies turn to mush as we slowly weaken from the inside. Too much gravity, and our physical bodies are slowly squashed by the invisible weight of the extra G's. Our bodies work best at 1G.

One of the reasons why gravity gives you strong muscles and bones, and zero gravity gives you weak muscles and bones, is because of resistance.

Movement involves work. We do "work" everyday in simple everyday activities, because our muscles and bones have to apply a certain amount of force in order to overcome gravity. Our muscles adapt by growing the muscle fibres to provide that force, and bones remodel themselves to provide the maximum resistance to the loads that gravity and the muscles put through them. We're not aware of this day-to-day because we never experience prolonged changes in our gravitational fields.

When we need to do more work than our muscles are accustomed to, our muscle fibres increase in strength, first as the nerve networks that supply the muscles become more efficient, then after about two weeks of ongoing training, the fibres themselves increase in size.[96, 97] The growth in muscle fibres is caused by three related factors: mechanical tension, muscle damage and metabolic stress.[97] Mechanical tension involves "force generation and stretch". In other words, the muscle fibres are stretched just beyond their usual capacity, and they actively fight against the resistance. This damages the weaker muscle fibres, which are repaired. The remaining muscle fibres are forced to adapt by growing larger because of the stimulation of growth factors.[97]

One of my favourite "Demotivator" posters says, "That which does not kill me postpones the inevitable."[98] Of course, the phrase that they've parodied is, "That which does not kill us makes us stronger." Why is there truth to that idiom? Adversity occurs when life circumstances come against us. In other words, adversity resists us. In the arm wrestle between adversity and overcoming, work is involved. We have to fight back. We grow when adversity pushes us just beyond what we have done before, stretching us. We may sustain some damage in the process, but that helps to reduce our weaknesses, and forces us into growth as we heal. When we push back against adversity, the "cells" of our character grow.

Sometimes we can go too far though. I vividly remember the pictures of the UK's Paula Radcliffe, succumbing to the gruelling hills and scorching Athens heat with only four miles left in the 2004 Olympic Marathon. Muscle failure from excessive stretch or excessive endurance parallels the allostatic load response, which is what people commonly referred to as 'stress'.

Scientific evidence that stress is positive

There have been recent studies in animals that demonstrate that the right amount of stress is physically as well as mentally enhancing.

Neurogenesis is the process of new nerve cell formation. Studies of rodents placed under intermittent predictable stressors showed an increase in neurogenesis within the hippocampus, which is the part of the brain related to learning and memory. Along with this enhancement of neurogenesis, the function of the hippocampus increased, specifically hippocampal-dependent memory, with a reduction in depression and anxiety-like behaviours.

In their 2012 review of stress and depression research, David Petrik and his colleagues noted that, "Contrary to stress always being 'bad', it has long been appreciated that stress has an important biological role, and recent research supports that some amount of stress at the right time is actually useful for learning and memory."[99]

Lessons from stress

So what can we learn from stress? How do we use the stress that we are exposed to every day to make us grow strong and durable?

Firstly, like the guitar string, we need to learn when we're in tune, at the peak of our productivity. Or like the car engine, we need to learn what it feels like to be in the power band. When we know where our sweet spot is, we can operate within it, achieving our best in life without doing ourselves harm. This is the first point that we need to identify on our own personal stress/productivity curve. This is the point of maximum productivity.

The other life principle to be gained from the car engine analogy is that not all of us are high performance engines. I would love to think that I'm a F1 racing engine–highly tuned, supreme power–but I recognise my limitations. I would even settle for a 5-litre V8, but I know that I'm probably more like a well-tuned V6. Sometimes we apply the most stress to ourselves when we try to drive in the power band of someone else's engine. We are who we are, and we need to accept that.

It seems logical that if too much stress is bad for us, then having little or no stress is good for us, but like the new guitar string analogy, minimal stress makes us unproductive. Like zero gravity on the body, little or no stress makes us weak.

We also need to understand that a bit more stress is ok. It's inevitable that we are going to be stressed beyond what we usually cope with at times. Without that challenge, there would be no growth.

Challenges usually hurt. You can't have growth without pain. In the muscle analogy, at the stretch at which peak growth occurs, muscle fibres tear and the lactic acid build up in the remaining cells can be very uncomfortable. The key is learning how far we can push ourselves before we start to falter and fail. This is the second point we need to discover on our personal stress/productivity curve. This is the point of maximum growth.

Once we understand our own individual points of maximum productivity and growth, we can use them as guides to our personal growth and achievement. Actually, I should specify that these are our starting points because as we face challenges and experience growth, the points will change slightly. We can remap those points and continue in our pattern of growth and development.

Pushing ourselves into just enough stress to achieve growth, then pulling back to rest and restore, is a pattern of growth that is seen in many facets of the natural world and the human body. Body builders and athletes use this method all the time in their training. They push themselves with more repetitions and heavier weights, or longer or faster runs, then they pull back to consolidate their gains. During our adolescence, our bodies naturally go through growth spurts—periods of rapid growth followed by a plateau, before the next burst of growth hormone hits us again. Tree rings demonstrate that growth and consolidation occur all the way through the natural world.

I call this the Stressed-Rest cycle. The studies in animals on neurogenesis strengthen the theory, because it was the animals that experienced bursts of stress that showed enhanced neurogenesis, memory and reduced depression/anxiety behaviours.

If you want maximum personal growth, constant stress does not help. There have to be times of rest. Some people think that rest time is wasted time, reducing productivity, but as explained, without rest time, productivity rapidly falls away. Without rest, stress goes bad, leading to allostatic overload.

So in summary, excessive stress is bad, but if all stress were bad, then we would all crumple any time that something became difficult. So stress is not a force for evil. Stress is part of our normal everyday lives, and is vital if we are to see ongoing personal growth.

We know from living life that we all don't fall in a heap when things go wrong. We have built-in ways of coping that help us to absorb troubles and adversities and like emotional photosynthesis—turn them into fuel for growth.

What is it that makes the difference between helpful and harmful? What is it that causes one person to surf the tsunami of sewerage that often confronts us in life, while another person sinks?

The answer lies in resilience.

Resilience

Resilience is the term given to the individual's capacity to cope.

Researchers in the field of psychiatry often use the term resilience, which they define as "the capacity and dynamic process of adaptively overcoming stress and adversity while maintaining normal psychological and physical functioning."[100]

Psychologists and social science researchers would use the term "coping", which also has several definitions, but for mine, the best one is "action regulation under stress."[101]

Big words sound impressive but to break it down, there are only two important things to remember about what resilience/coping is.

First, coping/resilience is an active process. It's not something that happens despite of us – we actively cope with stress. In the face of a situation involving emotional arousal (danger or stress), we take steps to deal with our inner and outer environments (the physiological processes of our body, as well as the environment around us).

Second, sometimes these steps are conscious and/or under our control, but theorists also consider automatic, unconscious, and involuntary responses to be part of the coping spectrum.[102]

What contributes to resilience?

What makes up those actions? What influences the action steps?

Coping Strategies

Psychologists have described hundreds of individual methods of coping through recent research. These coping strategies are simply behaviours and actions that people describe as ways they cope with different situations. Some of these strategies are taught to us by our parents, some we learn through watching others, and some we figure out ourselves.

As a practical example, let's take flat pack furniture. I dread my wife going to Ikea and bringing home some random set of shelves or drawers called 'Fyrkantig' or 'Straytphorwud'. Some of the instructions seem straight forward, but I inevitably get some obscure wooden connector thing backwards, or in the wrong order, or I accidentally use screw J instead of the nearly identical but critically different screw K.

There are different ways in which to cope with such flat pack fails. An adaptive coping strategy would be to pause, reread the instructions, and go back a step or two. Another might be to call a friend who is good with flat pack furniture to help. Another might be to watch a YouTube video of someone putting together the same item. A maladaptive, not-very-useful strategy would be to curse and swear at the half-built furniture and fantasise about using that annoying little allen key to murder the guy who designed the homicide-inducing pre-fabricated abomination.

There are literally hundreds of different ways in which individuals cope with things. Social scientists have further classified them into larger groups to try to make sense out of them. For example, in my flat pack fail example, rereading the instructions or asking another person for help might be considered to be "reading, observation, and asking others," which would then be classified with other similar strategies as "finding additional contingencies", which is grouped into an even higher general class like "Coordinate actions and contingencies in the environment."[101] (There are so many that it would be impossible to cover them all here, but if you want to know more about the plethora of different coping strategies, read the paper by social psychologists Skinner and Zimmer-Gembeck).[101]

Personality factors

Coping strategies follow along the lines of personality type[103] (and the stage of development in children).[101] Personality types such as Neuroticism and Openness have been well studied, with Neuroticism associated with maladaptive coping strategies, and Openness correlated with adaptive coping (in several areas including marital relationships[104] and in public speaking tasks[103]).

Further research has shown how personality significantly influences coping, with the severity of the stress, and the age and culture of a person influencing the strategy and strength of the coping response.[102] Of course, personality traits like neuroticism sound bad, but they confer their own strengths. For example, 'negative affect' has protective benefits by enhancing the detection of deception.[105]

Biological factors

Personality types and coping responses are connected because they both share common genes.[106]

Variations in individual genes effect the ability of the brain to associate the correct value to rewards, which then influences both mood and learning.[23, 107, 108] This fits very nicely with the CAP model that I discussed in earlier chapters.

Environmental factors also have a role in determining personality and how a person learns to cope with stress, though genetics modifies the effect of the environment to a point. Genetic variations alter how the brain perceives and processes these signals, so environmental factors are only as influential as the brain will allow.

On a deeper level, there are several biological processes that make up the features of resilience. Resilient individuals have the full complement of critical components in the resilience pathway, and have some extra tools too.[109] The key genetic variations increase the ability of the brain cells to grow new branches and form new pathways, and make the communication in the stress, mood and rewards systems more efficient and effective. Certain types of stress can enhance the activity of these genes, which can increase the protective effects of stress.[100]

While certain types of stress can be protective, other forms of stress can be particularly damaging, especially uncontrollable early childhood trauma.

Resilience on a personal level

Resilience factors, whether they be innate or learned, are protective for stress, and are more commonly deployed than we realize. Despite all of the publicity that stress has generated, human beings remain remarkably unscathed. It's estimated that between fifty and sixty percent of the general population experience a severe trauma at some time in their lives, yet serious repercussions like post-traumatic stress disorder occur in less than ten percent.[109]

As individuals, we naturally cope in different ways, often related to our personality style and our gender. It's a generalisation, sure, but commonly men tend to engage in "fight-or-fight" responses to stress where women usually move to "tend-and-befriend" mode.[110] In animal studies, the female animals coped better with chronic stress whereas the male animals coped better with acute stress.[109] Granted, we're not rats, so the research may not be directly applicable to us, but I still find it really interesting, and there maybe a lesson for us in there somewhere.

As a general rule, what's adaptive in some situations and for some people is maladaptive in other situations and for other people. This is where our personality often influences our coping, but not just our personality, but as I outlined in the CAP model, also our genes, our perception, and our physiology. Human studies on coping show that what is good for one is not necessarily good for another. People who are highly sensitivity to threat (anxious or wary) are often harmed by engaging directly with that threat, and often benefit from withdrawing in the short term. The opposite pattern is true for people who aren't as sensitive.[102]

The message here is just because being proactive and engaging may be a positive method of coping for some doesn't mean it should be recommended to everyone. Pushing someone to tackle their problem head on maybe more harmful than helpful, so care should be taken when giving people advice about how to manage their stress. Ill-informed instructions can sometimes make things worse.

Allostatic overload – Stress 'Breaking Bad'

One of my favourite shows of all time was Breaking Bad. Breaking Bad told the story of Walter White, a high school chemistry teacher and average family man who's diagnosed with terminal lung cancer. To support his wife and disabled son after he's gone, he uses his knowledge of chemistry to launch himself into an underworld career manufacturing crystal meth.

Allostatic overload is the term modern scientists use for stress breaking bad. Stress moves from an agent of growth and change to an agent of disease and death.

Earlier in the chapter, I discussed that stress is actually more of a positive than a negative. It's not that stress can't be bad, because we know from the stress-productivity curve and from the Yerkes-Dodson Law that too much stress overwhelms our capacity to cope with it. The model used to describe the balance of stress on our body is the theory of Allostasis.

All living things survive because of a delicate balancing of dozens of different internal systems, such as maintaining the right amount of blood sugar, maintaining the correct body temperature, maintaining the right pH balance of the body, etc. To work properly, each system often relies on all the other systems working at an optimal range.

Imagine trying to stack ten spinning tops on top of each other while trying to keep them spinning. The body does the chemical equivalent of this very difficult combination of balance and dexterity every day. It's called homeostasis. This balancing act is constantly challenged by internal or external events, termed stressors. Both the amount of stress and amount of time that the stressor is applied is important. When any stressor exceeds a certain threshold ("too strong, or too long"), the internal systems activate responses that compensate in order to maintain the optimal balance.

The theory of allostasis is related to these internal adaptive mechanisms, although not just in terms of stress, but broadly to the concept of any change of the optimal range of these corrective processes, in response to a change in the environment or life cycle of an organism.[111]

An example of allostasis in nature is the capacity of some bird species to change their stress response to facilitate their breeding capacity during mating season. The benefit of the increased chance of breeding is important to the bird, but also comes at a cost of increased susceptibility to some diseases because of the weakening of the stress response at the time.[111]

When it comes to stress, we adapt in a similar way. A lack of stress, or an excess of a stressor in some way (either too long or too strong) results in adaptation, which is beneficial, but can come at a cost. This is demonstrated by that broadly applicable U-curve, the stress productivity curve.

Our response to the stress can go one of three ways:

1. The adaptation to the stress may be perfect and our system returns to its normal operating conditions,

2. The adaptive response may be mismatched (for example, inadequate, excessive and/or prolonged) and our system suffers,

3. The adaptation to the stress may be a perfect match AND our system gains from the experience and a new, improved capacity to cope is attained.[112, 113]

More often than not, we adapt to the stressor, either the same as before, or possibly better. It's only if the response to the stressor is inadequate, excessive and/or prolonged that stress ends up causing us trouble. This is what people normally think of when they think of stress – called allostatic overload – which is simply stress breaking bad.

The Tap Model of mental health

So to summarise – our mental health is strongly influenced by the balance between stress and our ability to cope with that stress. We need stress in order to remain strong, to perform at our best and to fulfil our potential. Too much stress, or not enough factors to cope with that stress, throws out the balance, which can turn stress from an agent of growth and change to an agent of death and destruction because of system overload.

As complicated as our body is, many of the systems in our body are much the same way. We experience good health when our body's systems are able to cope with the demands placed upon them. Disease occurs when our body is unable to cope, because of too much demand on our body's systems, or because of normal demand and an impaired capacity to cope with it.

Take sugar for example. When we have a load of sugar, our insulin system kicks in, and the excess sugar is taken out of the blood stream and into the cells for either use or storage. If we were to have a single jelly bean, then that's not a high demand, and our pancreas could easily produce enough insulin to cope. Say we ate a whole jar of jelly beans; our pancreas would have to work a lot harder, but for most people with a normal pancreas, we'd still cope.

Broadly speaking, diabetes mellitus is a disease involving broken glucose processing. There are two main types of diabetes. In Type 1, there is an absolute lack of insulin – the body doesn't have enough insulin because it doesn't have enough cells to produce insulin. In Type 2, there is a relative lack of insulin – the body has lots of insulin but it can't work properly because the cells don't respond to it properly. Either way, a small amount of sugar, even a single jelly bean, results in a higher amount of sugar in the blood because there isn't enough insulin to cope with the demand.

Think about it in a slightly different way. Imagine you're sitting in your lounge room watching your TV, and you can see the screen clearly but can't hear the sound properly. There could be two reasons for this–

you've got the volume turned all the way down or you've got some cotton in your ears. There is an absolute lack of sound (no volume), or there's a relative lack of sound (normal volume but you're temporarily deaf from your misuse of cotton balls). Either way, you can't hear anything and you can't enjoy your show.

I like to visualise this as a sink and tap ('faucet' if you're American). Think of your bathroom sink. When you have some water coming out of the tap at a rate which can be drained by the sink, then there's no overflow, and the rest of the bathroom stays dry. The system is coping with the input, and there's no problem. But if there's too much for the sink to cope with, then overflow occurs. Water goes everywhere and things get all messed up. There's a couple of reasons why the sink doesn't cope–perhaps you've got too much water going in to it (absolute excess of water), or perhaps there's something blocking up your drain and the normal amount of water can't drain out of the sink fast enough

The Tap Model of Mental Health

Our mental health can be thought of like a sink and faucet. Like the water from a faucet, we each have a certain amount of stress flowing into our lives. Like a sink, we each have a psychological capacity to cope with that stress (like the size of the sink) and a biological capacity to process the stress (the size of the drain)

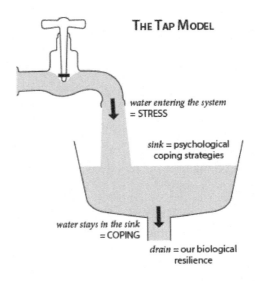

THE TAP MODEL

water entering the system = STRESS

sink = psychological coping strategies

water stays in the sink = COPING

drain = our biological resilience

(relative excess of water). It's also possible to have both at the same time. Either way, there's a mess.

This analogy applies to our mental health. The sink represents our coping mechanisms. The flow of water from the tap is stress. The drain is our biological resilience. Most people have limited stress, and robust biological and psychological coping systems – like having normal sinks and normal drainage, and a flow of water from the tap that can be easily dealt with by the sink.

Burnout, depression or anxiety can occur, however, when there's too much for the system to cope with. Perhaps it's because of a seventy-hour work week, or perhaps it's trying to juggle a demanding job, a busy family life, extra projects or further study. There's too much water coming into the sink and it eventually overflows. Sometimes the excess stress is from circumstances beyond a person's control, such as grief, personal trauma or natural disasters. When the excessive demands are removed, the system starts to cope again, and things return to normal.

The Tap Model – Too Much Stress

Too much stress entering the system is like too much water being poured into a sink – there is too much water coming in for the drain to process and the sink to hold, and water spills over the edge. Too much stress overwhelms the capacity to process it and cope with it, causing burnout

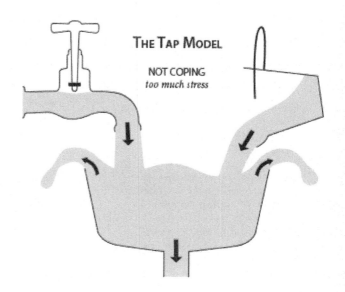

THE TAP MODEL

NOT COPING
too much stress

Then there are other people with biologically mediated depression or anxiety. They may have a normal amount of stress to deal with but their capacity to cope is limited. They may have poor coping mechanisms (a small sink) or deficiencies in their innate resilience (a small drain). Often, there's a combination of both. Either way, a normal volume of water from their tap would still overwhelm their system, and water would quickly overflow their sink and cause flooding. This is why some people seem to react poorly to what seems to others to be something trivial. It may be something minor but because they don't have the capacity to cope, or they're already at capacity, even the slightest thing seems to cause major flooding.

The answer is to either decrease the incoming water or increase the sink's capacity to cope. Different psychological treatments work in one of these two ways. 'Anti-depressant' medications like selective serotonin reuptake inhibitors work to increase the nerve cells growth of new branches,[114] which is like increasing the size of the drain pipe. Behavioural interventions like ACT or CBT help to increase the size

The Tap Model – Maladaptive Coping Strategie

Ineffective psychological coping strategies are like having a very small sink. Even a little bit of extra water can quickly overwhelm the capacity of the sink to cope with it, and the water spills over the edge. Ineffective coping reduces the capacity to cope with even small amounts of extra stress leading to anxiety and depression

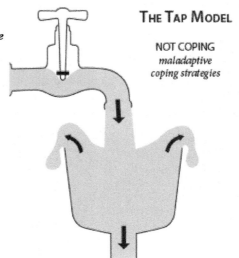

THE TAP MODEL

NOT COPING
*maladaptive
coping strategies*

The Tap Model –
Biological Factors

Deficiencies in stress and rewards processing in our brain (a small drain pipe) impairs our capacity to process the incoming signals from our environment. Extra stress is poorly processed and our psychological coping is quickly overwhelmed, leading to anxiety and depression

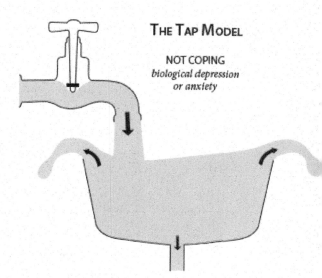

THE TAP MODEL

NOT COPING
*biological depression
or anxiety*

of the sink, so more water can be held in it. Some aspects of stress management involve learning to say no to things, and focus more on values, which helps to decrease the amount of stress coming into the system, effectively turning down the tap.

As we move into the rest of the book, and examine the different forms of mental illness, we will come back to look at both the CAP model and the Tap Model as ways of thinking about our mental health and wellbeing.

9

Burnout

Meet Jane

Jane was always a hard worker. She had a husband, two cats, and a house in the suburbs. Now in her mid-30's, she had worked for the same company since she left school, and had progressed up the corporate ladder through successive promotions to a middle management role.

Jane worked in the finance section, and while she had some quiet days, most of her month was very busy with a lot of work to get through each day. Towards the end of the month her workload would tend to peak. Her demanding job was also compounded by a redundancy of two key staff members, meaning that all of the other workers in her area had to share the extra load between them. When staff in her area went off sick, her workload would increase further.

It wasn't unusual that her 40-hour week would balloon out to 60 hours at the office, not including occasional work over the weekends. She was also trying to study part time to improve her qualifications so she could further climb the corporate ladder, with course work adding at least 10 hours a week.

In the last few months, she was noticing she was becoming increasingly irritable and snapping at people for small, seemingly trivial things, or she would just start crying for no good reason. She wasn't sleeping properly either. She would lay in bed thinking of all the things she would have to do the next day. When she did fall asleep, it was a light sleep where she would often toss and turn, and then wake up early in the morning, unable to fall back to sleep. She didn't feel like eating, but would sometimes become ravenous, and binge on fast food. Her concentration was becoming a problem at work as well, because it seemed to be taking her twice as long to work through her list of tasks. Her relationships were strained—her husband bore the brunt of her outbursts of rage, she didn't feel like sex anymore when she was home. She didn't really have much time for her friends either.

Jane was suffering from burnout.

What's burnout?

Burnout isn't strictly a formal psychiatric diagnosis. You won't find it in official classifications like the DSM-5 or ICD-10. Still, it's a very common term in our everyday language. People use the term "burnout" in many ways, from being just a little stressed, to having a mild nervous breakdown.

I think of burnout as the result of severe prolonged stress where all of our coping resources are utilised and overwhelmed. I also think of burnout as 'pre-depression', as burnout shares a lot of features of depression, but burnout quickly improves when the various sources of pressure are removed.

On the Stress-Productivity curve, we've moved beyond the point of maximal growth and are starting to slip down the other side. Or the guitar string—we've been wound a little too tight, and our note is starting to go off key, and a few fibres in our string are starting to break. Or thinking about the Tap Model, our sink is full but the water is still coming in, and we're spilling over the sides.

Why do we get burnout?

People experience burnout in real life when, like Jane, they're simply trying to cope with too much at once – they work long hours, they study, and they devote lots of time to church and ministry.

We want to do it all, and we try, but as individuals we're a finite resource, and we can only stretch so far. Eventually we become overstretched. We wear ourselves too thin and have nothing left to give.

There are many reasons for burnout, but one of the most common reasons: We don't say "no". There's a saying that "If you try to please everyone, you please no one." When we don't understand and practice our own values, we end up trying to live by someone else's values by default. Except that's like trying to wear someone else's shoes–they seem to fit, but never really fit properly. Remember, we all have different capacities and gifts. We have to be ourselves and work within the capacity that God has given us.

Sometimes we only have ourselves to blame, because in our enthusiasm, we can bite off more than we can chew. We take on too many responsibilities because we don't know our limits, or because we take on projects that don't align with our values, and we have to work so much harder to achieve them.

I have an amazing friend who I have known for many years. She has a phenomenal intellect. When we were medical students together, she would get distinctions and high distinctions without really trying that hard, while I had to work really hard just to scrape into a credit. Since graduating, she's written her own musical (as well directing it and starring in it), worked in TV, done consulting work for numerous medical and non-medical organisations on a national level, regularly runs workshops for doctors around Australia, trains new GP's, and much, much more. She is sharp, witty, creative, exuberant and nearly always happy. I wish I could be like her, but I'm not her. I could never replicate the things that she has done or could do. If I tried, I know I would simply set myself up for failure, and probably a nervous breakdown. I'm a Ford, she's a Ferrari.

I'm simply not gifted like she is. I don't have the same capacity. I have to embrace who I am, not try and be what she is. I have to trust God that he knew what he was doing when he made me who I am.

The symptoms of burnout are the similar to the symptoms of depression, which we'll discuss in more detail later. Burnout and depression share the same symptoms because they're on the same continuum, and are linked by the same neurobiology. In depression and burnout, the brain can not effectively grow enough new nerve cell branches to meet demand.[114] The difference tends to be in the cause. Depression tends to be biological and psychological, whereas burnout tends to be more environmental. The other difference is in severity, with burnout being similar to depression but on the milder end of the spectrum.

What's more important is that with burnout, the treatment is simply to remove the excessive load. Once this happens, the system can return to normal. On the other hand, depression is the result of deficiencies within the system itself, and while removing any excessive overload can help in cases of depression, it's not the only step necessary in management.

To remove that overload, you first have to take a step back, and re-evaluate things. Like an Olympic athlete, you have to remove all of the things that weigh you down and create drag. You have to try and do what is the most important things in the most efficient way, so you're not creating extra work for yourself.

Start by finding your values as we've discussed before, and set goals that fit with your values, not someone else's. And don't try and do it all, or try and do it all at once. Some stretching is ok, but you have to balance that out with rest periods or else you'll snap.

Keeping stress in check

Learning to say no, based on your values and subsequent goals, can greatly help to unload your life of unnecessary mass, but there are other ways to ensure that we keep our stress levels at the optimum to ensure maximum productivity and growth. Here are a few simple techniques.

Remember, everyone handles stress differently, and so which of these techniques works best for you will be something you'll have to learn by trying them.

Breathing

The simplest tool is breathing. Sounds a little silly really, because you obviously breathe all of the time, though we usually take shallow breaths, so our lungs are not being used to their full capacity. When we focus on our breathing and deliberately take slow deep breaths, we increase the amount of air going in, and therefore allow more oxygen to enter the blood stream. This better fuels our cells and helps them do their job more efficiently. It also sets in motion a physiological mechanism that slows our heart rate, however.

Our heart pumps blood from our body, through the lungs to get oxygenated. As we take a deep breath, more blood is sucked up into our chest cavity from our veins, because breathing in causes a temporary vacuum in our chest cavity. The extra blood then fills our heart more efficiently. A more efficient heart beat reduces the need for the body to stimulate the heart to pump harder and faster. This changes the balance of the activity between the two parts of our autonomic nervous system—there's more activity in the parasympathetic "rest-and-digest" nervous system, and less activity of the sympathetic "fight-or-flight" nervous system via a mechanism called the vagal brake.

To slow your breathing down, simply sit in a comfortable position. Take slow, deep breaths, right to the bottom of your lungs and expanding your chest forward through the central "heart" area. Count to five as you breathe in (five seconds, not one to five as quickly as possible) and then count to five as you breathe out. Keep doing this, slowly, deeply and rhythmically, in and out. Pretty simple! This will help to improve the efficiency of your heart and lungs, and reduce your stress levels.

Remember, B.R.E.A.T.H.E. = Breathe Rhythmically Evenly And Through the Heart Everyday.[27]

Meditation

Meditation takes the techniques of breathing one step further, in that meditation involves deliberately switching your brain's focus to something simple, and in the present. Focussing on nothing—just breathing and turning off your thinking for while—does take some practice. Concentrating on something in the present (not thinking about the past or the future), tends to be easier and requires less practice, although ignoring all the other thoughts that routinely clamour for your attention might be hard when you first try it.

Focusing on the present moment is part of the practice of Mindfulness. Mindfulness meditation has been studied quite extensively over the last few decades, and has been shown to have benefits over a large number of psychological symptoms and disease states.[76]

Sometimes it is easier to focus on something visual, that you can see easily in your field of view, or listen to something constant, like the ocean, or a metronome. The easiest thing to do is to again, focus on your breathing. Concentrate on the sound, rhythm and feeling of your breathing, but don't engage your thoughts. Meditation quietens the mind, which is excellent for reducing stress, and can help to revitalise and refresh your mind.

Guided Imagery

Guided imagery is a step along from meditation. Instead of focussing on something tangible, guided imagery lets you imagine that you are somewhere pleasant, relaxing, or rejuvenating. Some people describe it as a vivid daydream.

Get comfortable, close your eyes and start to breathe slowly and deeply. Once you begin to relax, imagine your favourite scene. It could be at the beach, or in a log cabin in the snow-capped mountains, or swimming in the cool waters in a tropical rain-forest. Whatever you choose, try to imagine the scene in as much detail as possible, and involve all five of your senses if you can, like, for example, the cool water of the waterfall on your bare skin, the sounds of the birds in the trees, the smell of the moss-covered rocks, the canopy of tall trees and vines split by the waterfall and stream allowing the sunlight to spill in to the forest floor. Enjoy the details and the relaxation that this brings. To "come back", some recommend counting back from ten, and to tell yourself that when you reach one, you will feel calm and refreshed.

Guided imagery allows you to actively replace the harassing thoughts of your daily routine with pleasant soothing thoughts. There's some early scientific literature suggesting effectiveness, although more research is required.[115, 116] Again, with practice, this can be done anywhere, and can be done quickly if you need a short break to unwind.

Visualisations

Visualisations build on the techniques of guided imagery, but instead of the rain-forest or tropical paradise, you imagine yourself achieving goals, which again could be anything from improving your health, closing that deal, or hitting that perfect drive from the first tee. Again, try to imagine the scene in as much detail as you can, and involve all of your senses.

A word of explanation: while it's a favourite pitch of life coaches and self-titled cognitive neuroscientists everywhere, there's no scientific evidence to show that visualising something will make you more likely to achieve it. The benefit of visualisation draws from the relaxation that comes from imagining that special something you desire to achieve or acquire. There's no secret here. Seeing that million-dollar cheque in your mind doesn't make it happen, although it might help you relax.

PMR

Progressive Muscle Relaxation, or PMR for short, is similar to meditation, except that you contract, hold, and then relax your muscle groups in turn. You concentrate on the feel of the tightening and relaxing of the muscles instead of, or as well as, your breathing. Like meditation, it can be done anywhere and involves very little training.

The contraction of the muscle groups, beginning in your feet—working your way up the calves and thighs, tummy, chest, arms and neck, sequentially pumps all of the blood back towards your heart, giving you a boost of blood flow to your lungs. The deep breathing oxygenates this extra blood and hence, gives your brain a burst of oxygen.

Using PMR to meditate helps engage the vagal brake, and there is some evidence that it helps to reduce persistent pain.[117, 118]

Exercise

Exercise releases stress and enhances your physical health.[119, 120] It's flexible and easily adaptable. It can be done for free and without any specific equipment. The downside is that it is not possible everywhere (you can't go jogging in a plane), but as a daily discipline, it will enhance your physical and emotional wellbeing.

The benefits of exercise are firstly physical. It gets your heart pumping, the blood flowing and your lungs working to their full capacity. It builds physical fitness, which is important to enable the heart and lungs to work efficiently at all times. Exercise has effects on mood, improving depression[121] and anxiety.[122]

It can also act as a form of meditation – the solitude of a run or swimming a few laps, concentrating only on the splash of your strokes or the pounding of your feet on the ground – is similar to meditation except that you're moving (whereas meditation proper involves being still and relaxed). The outcome is much the same, and stress is often reduced by a session of physical exercise.

Music

Music is almost as fundamental to human existence as breathing, and it's almost as diverse as mankind itself. Listening to one's favourite music can enhance feelings of control and can increase pain tolerance and improve short term anxiety (stress).[123] The common characteristics of 'therapeutic' music is music that had less tonal (pitch) variation, less prominent chord changes, bass lines, or strong melodies.[124] The key element overall, however, was personal preference, as some of the participants in the study chose music like Country and Western or music of bands like Metallica.

The Bible teaches us to praise and worship God. In modern times, the Christian church has been blessed by the sheer abundance of worship songs and CD's, from some of the pioneers like Maranatha Music and Vineyard through to contemporary forces like Hillsong, and the new wave of worship through bands like Jesus Culture. Contemporary gospel music gives Christians a vehicle that promotes biological and psychological benefit and spiritual empowerment at the same time.

Massage

I love massage! The first time I had a proper massage was in the small city of Launceston in the tiny Australian state of Tasmania. After just 30 minutes of the therapist kneading my muscles with her iron fingers I felt so relaxed that when I sat up, I was light-headed. My heart rate and blood pressure had reduced so much that it took me a while before I could stand up properly!

Deep pressure massage has also been shown to help release the vagal brake enhancing the activity of the parasympathetic (rest-and-digest) part of the autonomic nervous system. There is good evidence of this effect in pre-term infants.[125] The evidence for adults isn't so strong, although that's probably because of a lack of quality research.[126] The good studies that have been done show a reduction of cortisol, blood pressure and heart rate after massage, with some studies showing small persistent effects.[126]

The data might be thin, but there is enough evidence to make it worth trying at least once.

Probiotics

I add probiotics to this list as a reference for the future. There's good evidence of the anxiety-reducing effect of a friendly bacteria garden in your intestines that interacts with your gut and your immune system in positive ways. Though there is, at this point, very little in the way of good quality human clinical trials. And we still don't know exactly which strains of probiotics are the most helpful for different conditions.[127, 128] But, given that they're unlikely to be harmful, it may be worth trialling a course of probiotics, and see how you feel in 30 days.

Work life balance

While the specific techniques that we've just discussed are all helpful in managing stress as it appears, good stress management is both reactive and proactive. We can reduce our overall stress levels more systematically by finding the optimal balance of work, ministry, and everyday life. This holistic approach to stress management forms the concept of work life balance.

I have three rules for good work-life balance.

1. The Triple-8 Rule

The Triple-8 Rule is: "8 hours work, 8 hours sleep, and 8 hours rest and recreation make up the 24 hour day."

For the purposes of this rule, 'work' includes paid and unpaid work and study. Think of 'work' as 'anything that makes you feel *less refreshed* than you felt before you started'. 'Rest and recreation' is the opposite of work.

Rest and recreation is 'anything that makes you feel *more refreshed* at the end than you felt at the beginning'.

As an example, some people love gardening. They love being outside in the fresh air, on their knees in the dirt, weeding and fertilizing, knowing that come spring they will have a lawn like a carpet framed by a floral tapestry. Despite it being physically demanding, they feel more relaxed and invigorated for their few hours in the garden. For them, gardening is rest and recreation. Personally, I hate gardening. I could think of nothing worse. I'm a Darwin-style gardener... it's survival of the fittest for the plants in my garden! Gardening would suck the life out of me, so for me, gardening would be work.

2. The Sabbath Rule

The Sabbath Rule is: "If God rested on the seventh day, then so should you."

This isn't meant to be sacrilegious. Nor is it meant to be taken as a binding, legalistic command that we're not allowed to work on a Saturday or a Sunday. It's simply an observation of the time-honoured Biblical principle of the Sabbath.

God worked six days and rested. God didn't rest because he was fatigued, but he rested because he was defining a pattern for humans to follow, which he enshrined in the Mosaic laws. Abstaining from work gave the Israelites an opportunity to refresh their physical bodies as well as a chance to engage with God and with their families. The Sabbath enriches our body, soul and spirit.

Whatever your schedule, make sure you abstain from work at least one day a week. (Remember, work is 'anything that makes you feel *less refreshed* than you felt before you started'.)

3. The Holiday Rule

The Holiday Rule is: "Take at least two weeks holiday every year."

We have the Holiday Rule because we need extended R&R to further refresh our bodies and minds. A study of more than 12,000 middle-aged men over the course of a decade showed that annual vacations were associated with a decrease risk of death, especially from heart attacks.[129]

When we have an extended time of rest and recreation, our stress hormones have a chance to rebalance. To achieve this state of renewal, we need at least 10 days of R&R in a row, but a full 14 days is better. So having a few four-day weekends scattered throughout the year isn't enough – you need two weeks as a block (and more if you can)!

Two weeks off a year still gives you fifty weeks to be productive, and if you have those two weeks off, you'll find that your fifty weeks will be more productive than a full year without a break.

Again, a reminder that rest and recreation is 'anything that makes you feel *more refreshed* at the end than you felt at the beginning'. Tearing around the country sight-seeing may be your idea of relaxation, but if you try to pack too much in, you may find yourself needing a holiday after your holiday. Remember, the key here is balance.

Conclusion

Burnout is a common presentation even though it's not an official diagnosis. It occurs when we're overloaded and our coping systems are overwhelmed. This leads to depression symptoms, but when we take the pressure off ourselves, our systems return to normal.

The key to preventing burnout is to set manageable goals that fit our values, and to remove all of the extra things that cause drag and add extra work when we don't need it. We also need to learn to cope better, and there are many simple ways that we can do this.

10

Depression

M^{eet Jason.}

Jason was the sort of guy that people always looked up to. By his late 20's, he had a law degree and was being groomed for an associate position in an international law firm. He was a naturally gifted leader and public speaker. He was talented at most sports and kept pretty fit, so he wasn't hard on the eye either. He helped lead the young adult's ministry at his church, and was often invited to speak from the pulpit, regularly leading the communion during the Sunday services, and even giving the occasional sermon.

Then, he started to change. It started with fatigue. He felt like he was always tired, no matter how much he slept. Then he started to feel like there was no joy in anything. It wasn't that he was sad, but there was no happiness either. After a couple of months, he started to get really irritable. He was able to mask it at church and work, but when he got home, it all flooded out. His wife bore the brunt of his moodiness and anger, which put a strain on their marriage.

After a while, he found it much harder to concentrate at work and church. He couldn't hide the emotional pain any more, and it became much easier to avoid social situations so he didn't have to always hide his distress. He stopped going to the young adult's services, and rarely made it to Sunday church. He still went to work every day but begrudgingly, more because he needed the money than because he wanted to go.

At times, the emotional pain he felt weighed so heavy on him that he literally felt like there was a weight in his chest. At his worst, he couldn't sleep more than four hours a night. He couldn't fall asleep for hours, and despite how tired he was, he would always wake up before 5am. He was always hungry but all he wanted was fatty or sugary foods, so he gained a lot of weight. He started drinking alcohol every night. He would burst into tears, seemingly for no reason. He hated himself. He knew the scriptures about how he was supposed to have the joy of the Lord, which made him feel like even more of a failure, as a Christian and as a person. Sometimes he even questioned whether God existed.

The despair Jason was enduring was depression.

What's depression?

Simply put, depression is an abnormally low mood for an abnormally long time.

Many people, both in the church and outside it, still think that depression is just letting yourself feel miserable. People without depression think that people with depression are weak, malingering, or wallowing in child-like self-pity. Despite the enormous strides in mental health education and awareness that have been made in the last couple of decades, there's still a strong current of stigma that flows through our society, adding an additional barrier to improvement for anyone living with or recovering from depression.

Depression affects, incidentally, a lot of people. The lifetime prevalence (how likely you are to suffer from depression at one stage through your life) is about twenty-five percent, or about one in four people. The point prevalence (those who are suffering from clinical depression at any particular time) is about six percent. I used to attend a church that had a regular congregation of about 2500 people. So statistically, one hundred and fifty people in that congregation are suffering from depression every Sunday, and more than 600 will experience depression in their lifetime.

What are the symptoms of depression?

As I said before, depression can be thought of as an abnormally low mood for an abnormally long time.

So it's more that just feeling sad, or bored. It's more than having occasional thoughts of dying.

To be officially classified as having depression, five (or more) of the following symptoms must be present during the same 2-week period and represent a change from previous functioning.

At least one of the symptoms is (1) depressed mood or (2) loss of interest or pleasure.

(1) Depressed mood most of the day, nearly every day.

(2) Markedly diminished interest or pleasure, most of the day, nearly every day.

(3) Significant weight changes or changes in appetite nearly every day.

(4) Unable to sleep or abnormally excessive sleeping, nearly every day.

(5) Agitation or dullness in the mind and body, nearly every day.

(6) Fatigue or loss of energy nearly every day.

(7) Feelings of worthlessness, or a feeling of guilt which is excessive or inappropriate nearly every day.

(8) Diminished ability to think or concentrate, or indecisiveness, nearly every day.

(9) Recurrent thoughts of death (not just fear of dying), recurrent thoughts of suicide without a specific plan, or a suicide attempt or specific plan for committing suicide.

Importantly, the symptoms cause significant distress or impairment in social functioning, at work, or other important areas, and the symptoms are not due to a medication or a medical condition (an underactive thyroid, for example).

What causes depression?

Depression has a number of causes and correlations. People who are chronically unwell, whether from chronic pain, long term illness such as cancer or autoimmune disease, or life threatening illnesses such as heart attacks or meningitis, have a higher rate of depression. People who have experienced significant physical or psychological trauma also have a higher rate of depression. In fact, stress of any form is highly correlated with depression (that is, people who suffer from any severe stress are more likely to develop depression).

This observation led to a theory about the development of depression called the Stress Exposure Model.[130] It suggested that you only develop depression because you've suffered from stress.

This is one of the most common assumptions about depression in our society, and there are some important consequences from this line of thinking. Like, if being stressed is the cause of depression then the cure for depression is simply reducing stress. This is probably why most people assume that depression is a choice, or a simple weakness, and why depressed people are often told to just snap out of it.

But there's more to depression than stress. Going back to the Tap Model from Chapter 8, depression is a balancing act between the demands on the brains processing, and its capacity to meet those demands. So some depression is predominantly biological, which is the equivalent in the Tap Model of having a small sink and a small drain. People with biological depression can't effectively deal with even a normal amount of demand on their system, because their brain doesn't have the resources to process the incoming signals correctly or efficiently.

The main biological cause is a deficiency of a growth factor called BDNF, which is needed for the nerve cells to grow new branches, which enable the brain to process new information. This theory is called the Neurotrophic Hypothesis of depression[131] ('neuro' = nerve and 'trophic' = growth). BDNF isn't the only critical factor in the biological story of depression. There are many others, including the stress hormone system,[132] the serotonin system[22] and the dopamine/rewards system.[23]

Some depression is predominantly psychological. In the Tap Model, this would be the equivalent of having a bucket of water being dumped into the sink all at once, or having a very small sink that can't hold a lot of water. There are certain situations in which there is so much going on and so much change and adaptation is required that the brains coping systems simply can't cope. For example, people who have suffered severe and sudden traumas such as natural disasters (earthquake or flood victims), or personal tragedies like a massive house fire or an assault.

I also think grief is in this category, although I need to make it very clear that normal grief is NOT depression. Grief is a normal life experience, the psychological equivalent to wound healing.[133] Even though grief and depression are very similar in how the symptoms manifest, grief is not a disease process. Grief and depression seem similar because grief is a sudden demand on the brain's ability to adapt and cope, and the brain can only process so much at one time.

Most of the time, depression is a combination of both biological and psychological. In terms of the Tap Model, the sink is small, the drain pipe is clogged, and we've opened up the tap too much to allow too much water to gush in. Eventually, the water overflows. In depression, genetic factors determine our capacity to handle the incoming stressors. The nerve cells may not have enough BDNF and are slow to grow new branches. Genetics are also important in determining other mechanisms of resilience, and people with poor resilience are also more prone to depression.[100, 109, 134] Genetics also influence other factors such as our personality. People with the neurotic personality type, classically the introvert-pessimist sort of person, are more prone to depression, because of the way their brain naturally biases the flavour of the incoming information.[135] What is also very interesting is that these tendencies to depression also tend to create more stress.[130, 136] So stress is important to the risk of depression, but ironically, it's the risk of depression that influences the risk of stress not the other way around.

The risk of depression is related to an increased tendency towards stress, and poor processing of that stress because of personality factors and a reduced capacity to cope. All three of these factors are influenced by a broad array of genetic factors.

What's also important to see here is that being depressed isn't because of "toxic thinking" or because of "negative confessions". What we say and what we think are signs of what is going on underneath, not the cause of it. Conversely, you can make as many faith-filled confessions as you like, but if they don't help you to change your capacity to cope, then they're just hot air.

How do you manage depression?

Going back to the Tap Model, if the system is failing because of increased demand or decreased capacity to cope, then it's logical to manage depression by decreasing demand and increasing capacity to cope.

We can increase our capacity to cope by increasing our brains capacity to grow new nerve branches, and to make the cells more efficient at doing their job.

More efficient, you may ask? How could our brain cells become more efficient at thinking? There is a general principle that applies to everyone's physical function, which is that better performance doesn't necessarily come from more cells, but cells that work better. When you go to the gym for the first time and start weight training, the initial increase in strength isn't from growing bigger muscle cells, but in making the existing cells better at what they do by improving their co-ordination.

Enhanced processing

When you want to improve the brains ability to do something (doing some 'mental weight training'), practicing that mental activity makes specific nerve cells in the brain fire in the same sequence each time. Each time they fire in the same sequence, the nerve cells grow new branches and connections between the nerve cells are strengthened. Each new branch and connection makes the nerve signal carried by those nerves cells stronger and stronger, and stronger signals carried makes the action mediated by that nerve pathway easier and more efficient until it becomes a habit. Once a habit is formed, you can perform the same action with very little, if any, conscious effort.

So, back to the new branches and the better efficiency. Increasing the growth of new nerve cell branches and connections (in science speak–

'synaptogenesis') involves increasing the growth factors. BDNF has been proven to be increased by anti-depressant medications[131, 137] and by exercise,[121, 134] both of which have been shown to improve the symptoms of depression. There may be some evidence that diet might improve depression in a similar way although the evidence is weak,[138] so we should take that with a grain of salt. In this sense, it appears that when our brain is able to more efficiently process the incoming signals, there is less distress. This is like making a bigger outlet pipe for our sink so the water can flow more freely.

Increasing capacity to cope

The next way of managing depression is to increase the capacity to cope—to develop a bigger sink, so to speak. The way we do that is through psychological therapies. There are several styles of psychological therapies, too many for me to discuss them all here. In the real world, most psychologists use a mix of a number of techniques that they tailor to the needs of their patient. I'm going to quickly outline the three most commonly used therapies.

Cognitive Behavioural Therapy, or CBT for short, is "based on the theory that emotional problems result from distorted attitudes and ways of thinking that can be corrected. The aim is to treat difficulties by problem solving, finding better strategies for coping, and overcoming irrational fears."[139] Essentially it is the combination of two different therapies, Cognitive therapy, and Behavioural therapy. Cognitive therapy, as the name suggests, assumes that people have mental health problems because of patterns of irrational thinking. Behavioural therapy is quite broad, but looks to challenge the thinking patterns with action (for example: gradual exposure to something a person is afraid of).

CBT is the most well researched form of psychotherapy, and has a lot of evidence for it's effectiveness,[73] though there's good evidence that it's the behavioural arm that gives it any clout.[140, 141] Trying to change your mental health just by trying to change your thoughts is generally ineffective.

In the last couple of decades, a new wave of psychological therapies has emerged from this idea that Cognitive Behavioural Therapy is just Behavioural Therapy with bling. The most notable is Acceptance and Commitment Therapy. We discussed ACT in detail in Chapter 6. ACT "is a psychological therapy that teaches mindfulness ('paying attention in a particular way: on purpose, in the present moment, non-judgementally') and acceptance (openness, willingness to sustain contact) skills for responding to uncontrollable experiences and thereby increased enactment of personal values."[142] ACT is different to CBT in that ACT doesn't rely on the idea of changing thoughts, but on simply accepting them.

Remember that according to ACT, you don't have to change your thoughts, because thoughts aren't that powerful to begin with—they're just words. Sometimes they're true, and sometimes they're helpful, but if we spent all of our time trying to fight them, we miss out on experiencing the joy in the present moment, and we can lose sight of the values that guide us into our future fulfilment.

The other common psychotherapy is Interpersonal Psychotherapy, also called IPT.

IPT "is concerned with the 'interpersonal context'—the relational factors that predispose, precipitate and perpetuate the patient's distress. Within IPT interpersonal relationships are the focus of therapeutic attention as the means to bring about change, with the aim of helping patients to improve their interpersonal relationships or change their expectations about them. In addition, the treatment also aims to assist patients to improve their social support network so that they can better manage their current interpersonal distress."[143]

In other words, mental distress of a person is reduced when the breakdown in the relationships of the person are identified, and the person is given skills to improve their relationships.

The common link between the three common forms of psychotherapy, CBT, ACT and IPT, are that their therapeutic effect comes from improving skills in different areas that the patient lacks. That is, psychological therapies increase the capacity of the patient to cope with things that they otherwise would not have handled well.

Decrease demand

The last way to manage depression is to limit the excessive demands that have been placed on the system in the first place. In the Tap Model, the idea is to turn down the flow of water from the faucet until it reaches a manageable level that the rest of the system can cope with. In real life, this is the ability to reduce the unnecessary stressors. People who are depressed tend to be bad at this, but there are a few basic skills that are common to all stress management techniques that can form the platform of ongoing better skills in this area.

We discussed these in more detail in the last chapter on burnout, so I won't go through them all again. I will give you one more exercise to do that can help bring our attention away from the intrusive thoughts of our internal world, back to the present moment. It probably has lots of names but I call it the count-down exercise.

'5 4 3 2 1'

The premise is simple – name five things you can see, four things you can touch, three things you can hear, two things you can smell and one thing you can taste.

So for example, sitting here in my home office, while typing this book onto my computer, I can see:

1. My desk lamp

2. My unopened mail

3. My mobile phone

4. My empty drink glass, and of course,

5. My computer

Ok, four things I can touch:

1. My keyboard

2. The chair under my butt

3. My clothes

4. Floor under my feet

Ok, three things that I can hear:

1. Air conditioning

2. Some people talking as they're walking past my house

3. Hmmm... my wife and kids are in bed, so it's actually pretty quiet ... actually, I can hear the keys as I'm typing on them on my keyboard...

Ok, two things I can smell and one thing I can taste... this group is always the trickiest:

1. I can still taste the drink I had a few minutes ago – a cup of tea.

2. Every now and then, there's a hint of vanilla from a scented oil burner my wife is partial to ...

Umm ... I think that's it ...

It's good practice to try and get the full number for each sense, but don't worry if you can't. The point of the exercise isn't about getting some magic number of things, it's about getting you out of your own head and into the present moment. This helps us to move away from fighting our thoughts and gives us an appreciation for what's going on around us.

To recap, there are three main ways to manage depression–increase the brains ability to process the incoming emotional information, increase the capacity to cope, and decrease the amount of stress that our brains have to process.

Prayer

The fourth way to help manage depression is prayer. There is limited scientific information on the effects of prayer on depression, although a small randomised controlled trial did show that prayer with a prayer counsellor over a period of a number of weeks was more effective than no treatment.[144] But the Bible encourages us, "Do not be anxious about anything, but in every situation, by prayer and petition, with thanksgiving, present your requests to God. And the peace of God, which transcends all understanding, will guard your hearts and your minds in Christ Jesus." (Philippians 4:6-7)

And Jesus himself called to those heavy in heart, "Come to me, all you who are weary and burdened, and I will give you rest. Take my yoke upon you and learn from me, for I am gentle and humble in heart, and you will find rest for your souls. For my yoke is easy and my burden is light." (Matthew 11:28-30)

How can Christians get depressed?

One final thought. There are those in the church family that find it difficult to understand how strong Christians can become depressed in the first place. The Bible says that the fruit of the Spirit is joy doesn't it (Galatians 5:22)? And doesn't 1 Peter 1:8 suggest that every Christian should be "filled with an inexpressible and glorious joy."

Christians without depression sometimes assume that Christians they know who are suffering from depression must be faithless failures. And it seems the logical conclusion to draw. If the fruit of the Spirit is joy, and you're not filled with joy, then you mustn't be walking in the fullness of the Spirit.

Yet when you look through the greatest heroes in the Bible, you see a pattern where at one point or another in their lives, they went through physical and emotional destitution. Sure, their lives had some pretty amazing highs, but they often experienced some amazing lows as well. Moses spent forty years in the wilderness, and when God appeared to him in the burning bush, he argued with God about how weak and timid he was (Exodus 3 and 4).

In 1 Kings 18, Elijah had just seen God rain down fire to supernaturally consume his sacrifice, capture and kill four hundred and fifty prophets of Baal, and watched God break the drought over Israel. Yet in spite of being the conduit of these amazing demonstrations of Gods awesome power, when Jezebel the evil queen threatened him, he ran for his life in a panic and asked God to kill him, twice, over the period of a couple of months (1 Kings 19).

Peter had spent three years with Jesus, the Messiah himself, hearing him speak and watching him perform miracle after miracle after miracle. Peter even saw the empty tomb first hand on the very first Easter Sunday, but still, he gave up on life with God and went back to his former occupation, which turned out to be lots of hard work for very little reward (John 21:1-3). We'll come back to Peter later on.

The same pattern is also seen in King David, Gideon, and a number of other great leaders through the Bible. The take home message is this: it's human nature to suffer from disease and dysfunction. Sometimes it's physical dysfunction. Sometimes it's emotional dysfunction. It's not a personal or spiritual failure to have a physical illness. Why should mental illness be treated differently?

As the stories of Moses, Elijah and Peter testify, being a strong Christian doesn't make you impervious to low mood or emotional fatigue. Hey, we're all broken in some way, otherwise why would we need God's strength and salvation? If you close your eyes, you don't see light, but the light doesn't go away. In the same way, being depressed doesn't stop God's love, it just makes it hard to experience it. Having depression simply changes your capacity to experience the joy and love of God.

In the 80's and 90's, a popular Christian musician was a man named Carmen. One of his best known songs had these words,

"When problems try to bury you and make it hard to pray, it may seem like Friday night, but Sunday's on the way!"

It's really hard when you're afflicted by the dank darkness of depression. It may feel like Friday night, in a hole, with no light and no hope. Remember, nothing will separate us from the love of God (Romans 8:35-39), including depression. You may not feel it, but God's love is there. And Sunday's on the way.

Conclusion

Depression is a common mental health condition that can have prolonged and devastating consequences. Depression is characterised by either a sadness or a lack of joy which are abnormal in their intensity and their duration, but also affects sleep, appetite and motivation. It is caused by abnormalities in genes which affect the brains ability to grow new nerve cell branches, and which also affect in-built coping mechanisms, so stress is both more likely to occur in people who are more prone to depression, and the stress is then handled poorly, overloading their emotional capacity.

The management of depression is three-pronged: to improve the brains ability to grow new nerve cells through exercise and/or medication, to learn new ways to cope with distress, and to decrease the amount of stress in the first place.

Christians are not immune to depression, and it's important for Christians to understand that Christians suffering from depression are not weak, or failing in their spiritual walk, or are unloved by God. The love of God is always present, even if they are unable to process it properly. As dark and dismal as depression can become, there is hope. It may seem like Friday night, but Sunday's on the way.

11

Anxiety

Meet Annie.

Annie was your everyday suburban mum. She had a station wagon, a mortgage and three young kids. People often said she was a bit of a control freak, though she just put it down to some perfectionist tendencies. Her attention to detail suited her chosen profession as an accountant. After she gave birth to her first child, she switched to some part-time bookkeeping from home.

She was always "sensible" with her money, a good habit that helped her pay off most of her mortgage and the kids school fees, as well as her regular tithe and support for her two children in Cambodia through *Compassion*. Now in her late 30's, she was pretty comfortable, without most of the usual stresses that would face the average person with three kids and a mortgage.

Except, for the last nine months or so, she always felt like something bad was about to happen. She could never put her finger on it, but she continuously felt uneasy. At first it wasn't much, but as time went on, she would notice a jittery feeling, and her heart would beat a little faster. She thought it may have been preservatives in her nightly glass of red wine but stopping it didn't make any difference. If anything, she got worse. She also stopped coffee and tea, which also failed to stop her growing feelings of panic. She would lie awake at night, thinking of all the things that could go wrong, and all the things she had to do to try and stop them. She tried to cope by making endless lists that soon took over most of her time. She had to triple check her bookkeeping work for errors, which slowed her down enormously, and just added more stress.

By the time she sought help for her anxiety, she was having full blown panic attacks, where all of a sudden, without any specific trigger, she would suddenly feel her heart beating out of her chest, and a crushing tightness around her ribs that made her feel like she couldn't breathe. She would break into a cold sweat; her head would spin. She felt like she was going to die.

What's anxiety?

When you say the word "anxiety," it can mean different things to different people. To a lot of people, being anxious is the same as being a little frightened. To others, it's being really scared, but with good reason (like if you were confronted by a very venomous snake).

Medically speaking, anxiety isn't just being frightened or stressed. After all, it's normal to be frightened or stressed. God made us so that we could experience fear, because a little bit of fear is protective. There are dangers all around us, and if we had no fear at all, we'd end up becoming lunch for a wild animal, or road kill. So there's nothing wrong with a little bit of anxiety, in the right amount, for the right reason.

But anxiety at the wrong time, in the wrong amount, can disrupt our day-to-day tasks and make it hard to live a rich and fulfilling life. That's the anxiety that we'll be talking about in this chapter.

What are the symptoms of anxiety?

The official description of pathological anxiety reflects this idea of the wrong amount of anxiety about the wrong things:

"... marked symptoms of anxiety accompanied by either general apprehension (i.e. 'free-floating anxiety') or worry focused on multiple everyday events, most often concerning family, health, finances, and school or work, together with additional symptoms such as muscular tension or motor restlessness, sympathetic autonomic over-activity, subjective experience of nervousness, difficulty maintaining concentration, irritability, or sleep disturbance. The symptoms are present more days than not for at least several months and result in significant distress or significant impairment in personal, family, social, educational, occupational, or other important areas of functioning." (This is taken from the beta-version of the latest World Health Organisation's diagnostic guidelines, the ICD-11, although at the time of publication, the ICD-11 has yet to be formally ratified).

What are anxiety disorders?

There are six main disorders that come under the "anxiety disorders" umbrella, reflecting either an abnormal focus of anxiety or an abnormal intensity:

> Panic Disorder (abnormally intense anxiety episodes)

> Social Anxiety Disorder (abnormal anxiety of social interactions)

> Post-traumatic Stress Disorder (abnormally intense episodes of anxiety following trauma)

> Obsessive-Compulsive Disorder (abnormally intense and abnormally focussed anxiety resulting in compulsive behaviours)

> Specific phobias (abnormally focussed anxiety on one particular trigger), and

> Generalised Anxiety Disorder (abnormal anxiety of everything)

What causes anxiety?

The common underlying theme of anxiety is uncertainty. Clinical psychologists Dan Grupe and Jack Nitschke from the University of Wisconsin wrote in Nature Reviews Neuroscience that "Anxiety is a future-orientated emotion, and anticipating or 'pre-viewing' the future induces anxiety largely because the future is intrinsically uncertain."[145]

The fear of uncertainty that defines anxiety comes from genetic changes that affect the structure and function of the brain, primarily in the regions of the amygdala and the pre-frontal cortex.

As a result of these changes, the brain processes information incorrectly. For example:

> the brain thinks that threats are more likely and will be worse than they are,

> the brain spends more time looking for possible threats,

> the brain fails to learn what conditions are safe, which is aggravated by avoidance, and

> the brain assumes that unavoidable uncertainty is more likely to be bad than good.

It's important to understand at this point that anxiety disorders aren't the result of poor personal choices. They're the result of a genetic predisposition to increased vulnerability to early life stress, and to chronic stress.[146] The other way of looking at it is that people who don't suffer from anxiety disorders have a fully functional capacity for resilience.[100, 109]

It's not to say that our choices have no impact at all, but we need to be realistic about this. Everyone will experience stressful situations at some point in their lives, and everyone will also make dumb choices in their lives. Some people are naturally equipped to handle this while some people have genes that make them more vulnerable. It's wrong to blame yourself or allow other people to blame you for experiencing anxiety, just as it's wrong for other people to assume that if one person can cope with a particular level of stress, then everyone else should too.

And it's not to say that you can't fight back. Just because you're facing a mountain doesn't mean to say you can't climb it. It will be hard work, and you'll need good training and support, but you can still climb that mountain.

How is anxiety managed?

Managing anxiety is very similar to managing depression like we discussed in the last chapter. Following the Tap Model, there's overflow when there is too much going into the system, the system is too small to handle it, and the processing of the input is too slow. So managing anxiety involves reducing the amount of stress going into the system, increasing the system's capacity through learning resilience and coping skills, and sometimes by improving the system's processing power with medications.

Reducing the input—stress management

Sometimes the best way of coping with anxiety is to reduce the stress that's fanning the flames. It mightn't seem to come naturally, but as we discussed in chapter 9, there are a few basic skills that are common to all stress management techniques that can form the platform of ongoing better skills in this area.

Engaging the "vagal brake" as proposed by the "Polyvagal Theory"[147] is as important in anxiety as it is in depression. By performing these techniques, the activity of the parasympathetic "rest-and-digest" nervous system is increased, which not only slows down the heart, but enhances the activity of other automatic parts of our metabolism. Some of the techniques allow a relaxed body to have a relaxed brain, which can cope better with whatever is confronting it.

The simplest techniques can be done any time, any where—don't forget to BREATHE (Breathe Rhythmically Evenly And Through the Heart Everyday) and the '5 4 3 2 1' exercise. Now might be a good time to go back to chapter 9 and recap.

Increasing capacity—coping and resilience

Like with depression, anxiety responds well to psychological therapies which help to increase coping skills and enhance our innate capacity for resilience, like CBT and ACT.[148, 149] ACT and CBT both enhance the activity of the pre-frontal regions of the brain.[150]

For anxiety, CBT teaches new skills to handle uncertain situations, and to re-evaluate the chances of bad things happening and what would happen if they do. ACT puts the train of anxious thoughts and feelings in their place, and teaches engagement with both the present moment and a future focusing on values while accepting the discomfort of uncertainty by removing the distress associated with it.

Practicing each of these skill sets is like practicing any other skill. Eventually, with enough practice, they start to become more like a reflex, and we start to cope with stress and anxiety better automatically.

Enhanced processing

Sometimes, to achieve long-term successful management of anxiety, a little extra help is needed in the form of medication. Like depression, the main group of medications used are the Selective Serotonin Reuptake Inhibitors (or SSRI's for short). Medications like SSRI's appear to reduce the over-activity of a number of brain regions collectively called the limbic system,[150] which essentially controls many of our emotions and motivations, including fear, anger and certain aspects of pleasure-seeking.[151] So SSRI's help the anxious brain make better sense of the incoming signals.

There are other medications commonly used for anxiety treatment, collectively called benzodiazepines. Most people wouldn't have heard that term before, but would have heard of the most famous member of the benzo family, Valium. Benzos are like having a bit too much alcohol—they slow down the activity of the brain, and induce a feeling of relaxation. When used appropriately, in low doses and in the short term, they can be helpful in taking the edge off quite distressing feelings of anxiety or panic. But benzos are not a cure, and after a while, the body builds a tolerance to them, where a higher dose is required to achieve the same effect. Continued long term use eventually creates dependence where a person finds it difficult to cope without them.

Prayer

The final way to help manage anxiety is prayer. Like for depression, there's limited scientific information on the effects of prayer on anxiety, although a small randomised controlled trial did show that prayer with a prayer counsellor over a period of a number of weeks was more effective than no treatment.[144]

Though given that anxiety is a future orientated emotion, excessively anticipating possible unwelcome scenarios and consequences, it's easy to see why prayer should work well for anxiety. Trusting that God has the future in hand and knowing "that in all things God works for the good of those who love him, who have been called according to his purpose" (Romans 8:28) means that the future is less uncertain. The Bible also encourages us, "Do not be anxious about anything, but in every situation, by prayer and petition, with thanksgiving, present your requests to God. And the peace of God, which transcends all understanding, will guard your hearts and your minds in Christ Jesus." (Philippians 4:6-7) When we give the future to God, he will give us peace in return. We don't have to understand it (it transcends understanding, after all), we just need to accept it.

How could Christians get anxiety?

Again, like in the case of depression, it's sometimes hard for Christians to understand how someone who truly loves God can suffer from anxiety in the first place. After all, we've just read how God gives us peace, and the Bible says that the fruit of the Spirit is peace (Galatians 5:22).

So when you're filled with anxiety and all you feel is overwhelming fear, it makes you feel like a faithless failure. Christians without anxiety assume that Christians with anxiety aren't living in the Spirit, which is the logical conclusion to draw – if the fruit of the Spirit is peace, and you're not filled with peace, then you mustn't be full of the Spirit.

But like depression, when you look through the greatest heroes in the Bible, you see a pattern where at one point or another in their lives, they went through physical and emotional destitution, including mind-numbing fear. Remember Gideon? He was in hiding from the Midianites, threshing wheat in a winepress, and when God called him to deliver Israel, his reply was, "O my Lord, how can I save Israel? Indeed my clan is the weakest in Manasseh, and I am the least in my father's house." (Judges 6:15) Moses was just as timid when God called him from the burning bush, so much so that he argued with God himself, asking him to pick anyone to save Israel but him, "Then Moses said to the Lord, 'O my Lord, I am not eloquent, neither before nor since You have spoken to Your servant; but I am slow of speech and slow of tongue.'" (Exodus 4:10)

Remember, it's human nature to suffer from disease and dysfunction. Sometimes it's physical dysfunction. Sometimes it's emotional dysfunction. It's not a personal or spiritual failure to have a physical illness. Why should mental illness be treated any different?

Being a strong Christian doesn't make you impervious to fear and anxiety. Hey, we're all broken in some way, otherwise why would we need God's strength and salvation. Having anxiety simply changes your capacity to experience God's peace. As I said in the last chapter, closing your eyes doesn't stop the light, it just stops you experiencing the light. Having an anxiety disorder might make it harder to sense God's peace, but it doesn't stop God's peace, or his love for that matter: "Who shall separate us from the love of Christ? Shall trouble or hardship or persecution or famine or nakedness or danger or sword? ... No, in all these things we are more than conquerors through him who loved us." (Romans 8:35,37)

Conclusion

Some anxiety, at the right time and at the right intensity, is normal. It's not unhealthy or sinful to experience some anxiety.

Anxiety at the wrong time or at the wrong intensity, can disrupt our day-to-day tasks and make it hard to live a rich and fulfilling life. Anxiety is a future-orientated emotion. Anticipating or 'pre-viewing' the future induces anxiety because the future is intrinsically uncertain. Anxiety disorders can be debilitating.

Like depression, anxiety disorders can be managed in four main ways, by reducing the amount of stress coming in with stress management techniques, by increasing capacity to cope with psychological therapies like CBT and ACT, and sometimes by using medications, which help the brain to process the uncertainty of each situation more effectively. Prayer is can also be useful in helping manage anxiety.

Christians are not immune from anxiety disorders, and it's important for Christians to understand that other Christians suffering from anxiety disorders are not weak, or failing in their spiritual walk, or should "just have more faith". Having anxiety is not because of making poor choices. Though if you have anxiety, you can still trust in the promises of the Bible, that God has the future under control.

12

Schizophrenia

L et me introduce you to Pete.

Pete was always that guy at the back. He was quiet and a little quirky. He never really had a sense of fashion. He never really had a lot of friends. He liked people, but he just never seemed to click with anyone. At youth group, he always sat in the back row and worshipped quietly. After youth group and Sunday church, he would hang out with his group of friends but he always remained unobtrusive, generally preferring to be in the background.

Then one day, his friends noticed that Pete seemed different. He seemed more confident and bolder in his worship. His youth pastor was impressed by his new found passion. A month later, Pete told them he was planning to go on a missions trip instead of celebrating his upcoming 21st birthday, and started talking enthusiastically about church planting. He told them that God was speaking to him about growing God's kingdom.

It wasn't until a fortnight later when Pete started to talk about preaching the 'hidden' gospel that his youth leader and pastor started to have concerns. When they asked Pete about how he knew God was speaking to him, Pete said God was speaking to him through songs on the radio in a language that only he could understand. They offered him some counselling, but Pete was adamant that he didn't need counselling because God was talking to him.

A few days later, his youth leader got a phone call from Pete's housemate, who said that Pete seemed to be incoherent. When his pastor arrived, Pete was pacing frantically around the room. Pete was talking very quickly, and jumping from topic to topic. Pete kept talking about the voices of angels in his head, and the hidden gospel that he was called to preach. He wouldn't budge from the idea that the voices in his head were angels, or that God was communicating to him through the radio.

In medical terms, Pete was in the middle of his first episode of acute psychosis. Psychosis is one part of the complex disorder of schizophrenia.

What's schizophrenia?

Schizophrenia is one of the most maligned of all mental illnesses. Schizophrenia is the stereotypical form of madness. People think of schizophrenia as having a 'split personality', or label schizophrenics as deranged psychopaths who hear voices and commit mass murder. Many people think that schizophrenics should be locked away in padded cells and not come back out.

The 'positive' symptoms of schizophrenia–the hallucinations and delusional beliefs–often have religious content, so sometimes mild or early psychosis seems to be camouflaged by church beliefs and practices. (In saying that, I'm not implying that church beliefs and practices are a form of psychosis, although some church critics like to think so).

Schizophrenia seems quite rare. In reality, schizophrenia affects roughly one person in one hundred, but because of its pervasive nature, it remains in the top ten causes of disease burden around the globe. It usually manifests in the third decade of life (i.e.: young people in their

20's) although there is a smaller peak in women around the time of menopause.

Schizophrenia is a complex disorder of brain function. Despite amazing advances in our understanding of mental illness, there's still a lot that scientists don't know about schizophrenia. It has a wide variation in how it presents and progresses, so some researchers believe that what we currently lump together as schizophrenia may actually be a number of diseases that we don't have the technology to differentiate. What's more definitive is that the deficits in neurological function that manifest in the various syndromes of schizophrenia appear to have a number of genetic and environmental causes.

Symptoms of schizophrenia

As it currently stands, schizophrenia is defined in the DSM-5 as the presence of at least two typical symptoms, for at least a one-month period, which causes a significant impairment in either work, interpersonal relations, or self-care, and the continuous signs of the disturbance persist for a period of at least 6 months (prodrome, active phase and residual symptoms).

The typical symptoms of acute schizophrenia are: (1) delusions, (2) hallucinations, (3) disorganized speech, (4) grossly disorganized or catatonic behaviour, and (5) negative symptoms.

Delusions, hallucinations, disorganised speech and disorganised behaviour are all considered under the broad umbrella of psychosis, which is essentially a loss of contact with reality.

Delusions

Delusions are fixed, false beliefs that

1. are not widely held within the context of the individual's cultural or religious group, and

2. persist despite contradictory evidence or dysfunction clearly linked to the belief.

So to explain in a church context, Christians believe that the Holy Spirit speaks to people, either through the Bible, through worship songs, through sensations in the body, through confirmatory signs in the world around us, or sometimes as an audible voice. The experience of the Holy Spirit speaking or leading isn't a delusion so long as it fits in with the widely-held beliefs of the Christian church.

For example, if you saw a photo of your pastor on the church calendar on your fridge, and you felt the Holy Spirit prompted you to pray for him, then that's not a delusion, as it fits in with what the Bible says about the working of the Holy Spirit. It WOULD BE a delusion if you felt the Holy Spirit prompted you to (a) shoot your pastor, and (b) you couldn't be convinced that the Holy Spirit doesn't ask us to shoot people because it's inconsistent with the Bibles teachings.

There are many different forms that delusions can take, too numerous to list here. But common ones that appear in schizophrenia are:

Thought broadcasting: The false belief that a person's thoughts can be heard by others as if they are audible to everyone in their environment,

Thought insertion: The false belief that others are inserting specific thoughts into the person's head, or

Thought withdrawal: The false idea that people are able to intercept and remove a person's thoughts.

Hallucinations

Hallucinations involve hearing, seeing or sensing things that are not there. Again, true hallucinations differ from our own internal monologue or from experiences that we have sometimes when our mind plays tricks on us, because hallucinations appear to be external to the person experiencing them, and the person experiencing them believes they are a reality.

In schizophrenia, hallucinations are most commonly auditory, in the form of voices that keep a running commentary on everyday activities. They're sometimes unfriendly, insulting, or accusatory. Occasionally they take the form of commands, but people with schizophrenia usually don't follow through on those commands.

Disorganised speech or behaviour

Disorganised speech and/or behaviour reflects an underlying impairment in thought processes. The person with schizophrenia can't process stimuli accurately and is unable to link thoughts or ideas in a coherent and logical manner. There are many different varieties that are further defined in textbooks of psychiatry, but ones common to schizophrenia are *tangential speech*' where the speaker wanders from and never returns to the initial topic, *flight of ideas*' where the speech quickly jumps from one topic to another, and *word salad*', where the conversation is made up of random words strung together resulting in gibberish. Disorganised behaviour is similar to disorganised speech, but where actions are disjointed instead of words.

What's happening in the schizophrenia brain?

These symptoms of psychosis are related to an increased production of a particular neurotransmitter called dopamine in a part of the brain called the striatum. Dopamine is a critical neurotransmitter to the brain. Disruptions in the dopamine system are at the root of a number of different neurological conditions, including (but not limited to) Depression, Parkinsons disease and Attention Deficit Hyperactivity Disorder (ADHD).

Nerve cells in the striatum and other central parts of the brain use dopamine to communicate with each other. One function of the striatum and other central brain structures act like a relay station to deliver information to the rest of the brain.

Special delivery

Think of the brain as a giant mail delivery network. The function of the real-life postal service is to deliver packets of information in the form or parcels and letters from one place to another to facilitate communication. Well, the brain is a bit like that—packets of information need to be sent from one part of the brain to another to be processed or actioned. We like to think of our cerebral cortex, the thin layer of nerve cells on the outside of our brain, as the place where all the action is. The cortex is important for fine processing of information, but it's structures like the striatum, and other nearby structures deep in the brain, that ensures each packet of information is sent to the right part of the cortex, or to the other parts of the brain for action, like the spinal cord for movement. One function of the striatum is like the mail distribution centre—the central hub where the packets of information are sent to and then redirected appropriately.

The associative areas of the cortex are where the refined information from each of the three main senses (sight, hearing and touch) is sent to be constructed into a whole. Normally this information is sent from the striatum to areas of the frontal lobe to be slotted in to our world view. When the information from our association areas is balanced, each information packet gets treated with the importance that it requires. In psychosis, each information packet that's flowing between the striatum and the association cortex is given the wrong weighting. Or using the mail analogy, normal mail is given priority delivery. The thought processes of the brain then can't analyse the information correctly.[152]

The red ball

For example, suppose we see a red ball bouncing in front of us. Each component of that bouncing red ball is perceived by the eyes and ears, and processed separately at first. The colour, the size, the shape, the movement, and the tone and pitch of the sounds, are decoded by different parts of the cortex of the brain. As the pieces of the information signal pass through the brain, the different components are layered together as separate visual and audio information, then finally the audio and the visual components are brought together as the bouncing red ball.

But in order to make sense of this packet of information, the brain has to put it in context within our own personal reality. So the brain then compares the red bouncing ball to experiences we've encountered in the past; it attaches emotional information to the red bouncing ball, it decides what meaning the ball has at that moment and into the future and it formulates a plan of action in relation to the ball—"I like the colour red / this ball is really big to it must be an exercise ball / last time I tried to kick something this big I damaged the furniture so I'll pick it up instead / this ball shouldn't be in my lounge room in the first place, it should be in the spare room / it must be here because my children were playing with it again."

In psychosis and schizophrenia, the nerve fibres from the association cortex to the striatum release too much dopamine in response to information that isn't particularly important, so the bouncing red ball is given too much salience by the rest of the brain. The brain then tries to make the best sense out of it as possible, but the inferences the brain makes are not founded in reality–"The ball is really big / The colour red is the colour of emergencies / There must be a really big emergency happening / Someone must be telling me that there is a big emergency that I have to warn people about."

Negative symptoms of schizophrenia

The other part of schizophrenia that I haven't discussed yet is number five on the list of diagnostic symptoms–the so-called 'negative' symptoms. The word 'negative' has become associated with things that are bad, or toxic, or poisonous, but in the context of schizophrenia, 'negative' refers to 'lack or absence'.

Negative symptoms of schizophrenia follow on from the phase of psychosis, tend to last for much longer, and are usually much more debilitating. Typical negative symptoms include affective flattening (a markedly reduced range of emotional expression, seen as poor eye contact and reduced body language), alogia (also called 'poverty of speech', seen as brief or empty replies) and avolition (diminished goal-directed activities, such as going to school or work, or even self-care like basic hygiene).

Negative symptoms of schizophrenia are also related to dopamine dysfunction, but in the parts of the brain involved in computing rewards values for actions and their associated costs.

Areas in the brain called the orbitofrontal cortex, the ventral striatum and the anterior cingulate cortex are involved in calculating the reward values of possible actions, incorporating their costs and benefits, comparing any memories of previous similar actions to determine the effort required. This information is then used by other parts of the brain to assess all of the different possible actions, pick the best option and then carry out that plan.

Dopamine is necessary for this process, and the dysfunction of the dopamine system in schizophrenia interferes with the assessment of the effort and cost involved in each action.[153] The value of rewarding actions are discounted so they are perceived as less rewarding, and the perceived cost is incorrectly inflated.[154] In schizophrenia, this misattribution of rewards and costs is applied to nearly every action, and the result is very little action.

Cognitive impairment in schizophrenia

The other common finding in schizophrenia is cognitive impairment. Cognitive impairment is the inability of the brain to process new information, and is commonly seen in dementia. In schizophrenia, cognitive impairment is related to an increased function of dopamine in the brain. Working memory requires activity of the pre-frontal cortex, and the pre-frontal cortex requires an optimum level of dopamine from the striatal regions of the brain. Not enough dopamine, and too much dopamine impair the function the prefrontal cortex and working memory.[155] Schizophrenia is at the excessive end of the dopamine spectrum but the effect is the same as dementia caused by other dopamine-related diseases, such as Parkinson's disease.

What causes schizophrenia?

What causes the changes in the schizophrenic brain in the first place? It's theorised that schizophrenia is predominantly genetic,[156] but the genetic risk is triggered by external factors.[157] For example, it's known that problems during pregnancy such as low birth weight, Caesarean-section, infections during pregnancy and low oxygen during delivery are all associated with an increased risk of schizophrenia in later life. There are also links with social risk factors, such as growing up in a city, childhood adversity such as child abuse or loss of a parent, or even being an immigrant (with a much higher risk if you're easily identifiable as being in the minority).

These triggering events are all related to stress. Schizophrenia isn't a stress-related illness *per se,* but the pre-existing neurological differences from a persons genetic make up render them more vulnerable to stress. The more episodes of significant stress they're put under, the more likely they are to develop psychosis.[157] This may relate to another theory of the development of schizophrenia, that the neurological changes are enhanced by systemic inflammation and changes to the immune cells located within the brain.[158] One thing's for certain, there's still much to learn about the why of schizophrenia.

How is schizophrenia treated?

Even if we don't know everything about the why of schizophrenia, there are still good treatments available. The treatment for schizophrenia is slightly different to that of anxiety and depression, because the best treatments for schizophrenia are medications, especially for the initial phase of the disease involving the 'positive' symptoms.

Medications

Given that the fundamental cause of schizophrenia is an oversupply of the neurotransmitter dopamine, the medications for schizophrenia work by blocking the action of dopamine. The downside is that these antipsychotics do have some unpopular side effects. Dopamine isn't just used by the striatum to convey sensory signals to the prefrontal cortex, but also by other deeper parts of the brain (known collectively as the basal ganglia), helping to coordinate the smooth movements of our muscles among other things. The older antipsychotics would often push the levels of dopamine too low, which would result in tremors and other motor movement problems. They commonly led to weight gain (although the precise reason why this occurs is still largely unknown). The medications can also be quite sedating. These side effects are less with the newer antipsychotic medications, but they can still be unpleasant.

Despite their unwelcome side effects, the benefits of antipsychotic medications are undeniable. Two thirds of people with schizophrenia will respond to anti-psychotic medications, with remission or significant reduction in symptoms.[159] Antipsychotic medications reduce the recurrence of psychotic symptoms by nearly two-thirds, and result in improved quality of life.[160] Overall, treatment with antipsychotic medications reduced the death rate for people with schizophrenia[161] and also the rate of suicide.[162]

Talking therapies

What about 'talking' therapies such as ACT or CBT, that work in mood disorders like anxiety and depression? Do they work as well in schizophrenia? At this stage, there's no convincing evidence that CBT improves outcomes over being generally supportive.[163, 164] I suspect that this is because of the underlying cause of schizophrenia. In conditions like depression, the conclusions the brain makes are skewed because of emotional dysfunction, but the underlying thought process is sound. CBT and ACT help to correct the skewed conclusions by using the intact process of thinking to challenge dysfunctional emotions. Whereas in schizophrenia, the very foundations of the thought process are disrupted, so arguments to logic or the capacity to accurately re-evaluate your own thoughts are flawed from the get go. No matter how much you try, you can't think your way out of a condition where thinking itself is the fundamental problem.

Prayer

What about prayer for schizophrenia? There are very few published trials dedicated to the use of prayer in the treatment of schizophrenia. I could only find one that was done way back in 1979 and it lacked any statistical analysis of its data.[165] So I can't claim scientific confirmation of prayer for schizophrenia, but just as we have faith that God can heal our physical maladies, we can also trust him to heal our mental brokenness too. If you have the faith, then there's no reason not to try.

Conclusion

To sum up, schizophrenia is a common, debilitating, complex disorder of the brain that causes changes to the thought process of those who suffer from it, as indicated by delusions, hallucinations, disorganized speech behaviour, and negative symptoms. It's also associated with poor cognition relating to the dysfunction of the brains centres for working memory.

Schizophrenia is considered at this stage to be a disorder of neurodevelopment, and is related to a genetic susceptibility that's triggered by environmental factors. This results in excessive levels of the neurotransmitter dopamine in the deeper parts of the brain, which in turn, sends a skewed signal to the front sections of the brain for further processing. The skewed signals form the basis for hallucinations, delusions and other psychotic symptoms.

The best known treatment for schizophrenia is medication that blocks the excessive dopamine in the deeper parts of the brain. This is not without side effects, and not every person with schizophrenia will fully respond, but overall, functional capacity and quality of life are improved, and the number of relapses are lessened. The death rate is also reduced, including the death rate from suicide.

There's very little evidence of benefit from talking therapies in schizophrenia, and nearly no scientific evidence of the effectiveness of prayer, but there's no harm in trying them either.

With good support, most people with schizophrenia can enjoy meaningful relationships and occupations. It just requires a little bit of understanding on our part.

13

Attention Deficit Hyperactivity Disorder

Meet Ricky.

Ricky was a rambunctious tear away third-grader that didn't seem to have an off-switch. Like most boys his age, he loved to play. He loved to kick the football, climb trees, splash, swim, play tag ... he just seemed to go and go and never get tired. Ricky was like the Energizer Bunny plugged into the mains ... he just didn't stop.

To his parents, Josh and Suzie, that was the problem ... he just didn't stop. They loved the fact that he was boisterous and energetic outside, but Ricky was boisterous and energetic everywhere else too; at the dinner table, at the shops, trying to watch TV, and in Kid's Church.

Even getting ready for school in the morning was a monumental effort. Suzie was becoming increasingly frazzled because even the simplest of tasks, like putting his shoes on, required a prompt every thirty seconds to define the next step and to stay on task. It was the same for every other component in the process, like taking off his pyjamas, or putting on his uniform, or brushing his teeth. It took him forty minutes to perform a set of tasks that all the other kids his age need less than ten to accomplish.

At school, he was unable to sit for long enough to do a simple maths work-sheet. During story times, he would constantly blurt out answers or remarks. He'd fidget and squirm, butt into the games that the other kids were playing, and couldn't take turns. His reading was a full two year-levels below his peers, and at one point, his teacher thought he might have dyslexia.

Actually, Ricky had Attention Deficit Hyperactivity Disorder, or ADHD for short.

What is ADHD?

ADHD is a divisive, polarising topic. It's also the most common mental disorder in children, which makes it a really important topic to discuss.

There are lots of different misconceptions when it comes to ADHD:

ADHD is just an excuse for bad parenting.

ADHD is caused by sugar.

ADHD is caused by food colouring / preservatives / gluten / (any other fad 'toxin').

ADHD is cured by diet / meditation / herbal supplements / Swiss balls.

ADHD medication (Ritalin) is overused / a sign of lazy parenting / harmful / ungodly.

ADHD doesn't exist in France.

ADHD doesn't exist at all.

Society is slowly coming to terms with most mental illnesses, but despite being so common among the paediatric population, ADHD still lags way behind in the sympathy stakes. ADHD is the new AIDS. There is so much misinformation and discrimination surrounding ADHD in our modern 'enlightened' society that its stigma is worse than the actual illness, a testament to just how badly those with ADHD are marginalised.

One of the cruellest aspects of the cultural mismanagement of ADHD is the fact that it maligns the sufferers while simultaneously isolating them from much needed support. Saying that children with ADHD should just behave themselves, or parents of children with ADHD should just have better parenting skills is victim blaming at its worst.

Those people who believe that ADHD isn't a real disease also believe that ADHD is simply a mislabelling of normal energetic children who just need better structure, or better posture, or who learn differently. The truth is that those children who are more energetic, or who are 'kineasthetic' learners, do not fit the diagnosis of ADHD, at least not according to its formal definition.

How is ADHD formally defined?

The current criteria that must be matched to qualify for a diagnosis of ADHD is:

1. Inattention: Six or more symptoms of inattention for children up to age 16, or five or more for adolescents 17 and older and adults; symptoms of inattention have been present for at least 6 months, and they are inappropriate for developmental level:

* Often fails to give close attention to details or makes careless mistakes in schoolwork, at work, or with other activities.

* Often has trouble holding attention on tasks or play activities.

* Often does not seem to listen when spoken to directly.

* Often does not follow through on instructions and fails to finish schoolwork, chores, or duties in the workplace (e.g., loses focus, side-tracked).

* Often has trouble organizing tasks and activities.

* Often avoids, dislikes, or is reluctant to do tasks that require mental effort over a long period of time (such as schoolwork or homework).

* Often loses things necessary for tasks and activities (e.g. school materials, pencils, books, tools, wallets, keys, paperwork, eyeglasses, mobile telephones).

* Is often easily distracted

* Is often forgetful in daily activities.

2. *Hyperactivity and Impulsivity:* Six or more symptoms of hyperactivity-impulsivity for children up to age 16, or five or more for adolescents 17 and older and adults; symptoms of hyperactivity-impulsivity have been present for at least 6 months to an extent that is disruptive and inappropriate for the person's developmental level:

* Often fidgets with or taps hands or feet, or squirms in seat.

* Often leaves seat in situations when remaining seated is expected.

* Often runs about or climbs in situations where it is not appropriate (adolescents or adults may be limited to feeling restless).

* Often unable to play or take part in leisure activities quietly.

* Is often "on the go" acting as if "driven by a motor".

* Often talks excessively.

* Often blurts out an answer before a question has been completed.

* Often has trouble waiting his/her turn.

* Often interrupts or intrudes on others (e.g., butts into conversations or games)

In addition, the following conditions must be met:

- Several inattentive or hyperactive-impulsive symptoms were present before age 12 years.

- Several symptoms are present in two or more setting, (e.g., at home, school or work; with friends or relatives; in other activities).

- There is clear evidence that the symptoms interfere with, or reduce the quality of, social, school, or work functioning.

- The symptoms do not happen only during the course of schizophrenia or another psychotic disorder.

- The symptoms are not better explained by another mental disorder (e.g. Mood Disorder, Anxiety Disorder, Dissociative Disorder, or a Personality Disorder).

(http://www.cdc.gov/ncbddd/adhd/diagnosis.html)

There are several parts of this diagnostic criteria that are critically important in differentiating a normal but rambunctious child from a child with ADHD. ADHD requires that the symptoms are "disruptive and inappropriate for the person's developmental level," that they're "present in two or more settings," and "there is clear evidence that the symptoms interfere with, or reduce the quality of, social, school, or work functioning."

So ADHD is more than just being an active child who likes to play. ADHD is a dysfunctional lack of control that's abnormal compared to other children the same stage of development, is long standing and affects their entire lives.

These children find it hard to play with other kids because they can't follow the rules of their games or simply wait their turn, which is a basic social rule. These children find school difficult, because they can't concentrate for long enough to focus on completing a multi-step task, or they don't have a long enough attention span to make new memories for words or facts.

In Australia and in the UK, ADHD can't be formally diagnosed by anyone other than a paediatrician or a psychiatrist. The school counsellor or local naturopath can't diagnose it. Even as an experienced GP, I can't officially diagnose it. The diagnosis can only come from a medical specialist with at least a decade of university level training. The situation is slightly different in the US, where a number of health professionals can also make the diagnosis, including clinical psychologists and neuropsychologists, although only doctors can prescribe medication for it.

What are the causes of ADHD?

So why do some people develop ADHD? Like the other conditions that we've discussed earlier in the book, ADHD is believed to be a complex mix of abnormal genes activated by a cluster of environmental triggers. This process is currently described by the "Polygenic Liability Threshold Model."[166]

ADHD is known to be highly heritable, or in other words, there is a strong family link. First degree relatives (a parent, sibling, or child) of those with ADHD are two to eight times more likely than relatives of unaffected individuals to also have ADHD.[167] It's estimated that genetics contribute up to 76% of the development of ADHD.[168, 169] No one single gene seems to be responsible for ADHD. The hundreds of genes that are responsible have not been mapped with great certainty although this may be because studies have previously used small sample sizes and so have a low power for detecting what is likely to be a large number of genetic changes, each of which is responsible for a small amount of the development of the disease.[170]

There are a number of environmental triggers that influence the expression of the predisposing genes, most of which are related to pre-birth or early childhood. These include smoking during pregnancy, low birth weight, prematurity, severe maternal stress and early childhood adversity.[171]

At this stage, it's not precisely known how these factors cause changes in the brain. We do know that ADHD is commonly associated with other conditions including autism and anxiety,[172, 173] and anxiety and autism are understood to be the result of a fundamental problem in how certain nerve cells link with each other through the forming of synapses. So while not definitively proven, I believe that pregnancy factors or early childhood stress trigger the expression of specific genetic changes, which limit the nerve cells ability to grow new branches, especially in the areas of the brain involved in executive function, which we'll talk about momentarily.

What's better understood is that the neurotransmitter called dopamine is crucial to the ADHD disease process, since medications that flood the brain with dopamine significantly reduce the symptoms of ADHD.[174]

What's also understood is that children with ADHD have slower maturation of the grey matter[175] and structural changes in the frontal regions and deeper parts of the brain.[176] In more recent times, modern brain imaging techniques have been able to show differences in the way that the regions of the brain link together to form networks.

Think of the brain networks as a tug-o-war team. When all the members of a tug-o-war team work in unison, they increase their collective strength, but if the different team members don't co-ordinate their efforts properly, the strength is lost. The same goes for the brain. Modern neuroscientists have discovered that the function of the brain relies on physical networks within the brain, called "connectomes" and how these connectomes co-ordinate with each other.

In the ADHD brain, the connections between the different connectomes are immature.[177] These immature connections weaken the collective strength of the network, because they aren't synchronously "pulling" together.

So to summarise, ADHD is caused by an abnormal pattern of genes, the expression of which are triggered by environmental conditions in pregnancy and early childhood, resulting in slower maturation of the brain and an uncoordinated network of connectomes, which disrupts the attention and planning processes of the brain.

And I'll say this again, because it's important. ADHD is a disorder that is based on brain dysfunction. It's not caused by bad parenting or food additives. It doesn't matter how many times sanctimonious do-gooders lecture children with ADHD or their parents—lecturing doesn't help. ADHD is a brain-based disorder, not a matter of choice or training.

How is ADHD treated?

Medication

For the last sixty years, the most effective treatment of ADHD has remained unchanged. It's much maligned and stigmatised, but by far the most effective treatment of ADHD is stimulant medication.

It was in the 1930s that Dr Charles Bradley gave an amphetamine drug called Benzedrine to some severely disruptive, institutionalized, hyperactive boys. At the time, Benzedrine was promoted to stimulate the effects of normal brain function, but Bradley was using it for an entirely different reason, to try and reduce the headache that inevitably followed spinal tap procedures. It was one of those accidental discoveries that so often happens in science—the headaches didn't improve, but the boy's behaviour did.[178]

Bradley did a formal experiment on the effects of Benzedrine for the behavioural problems of children in 1937. He noted that half of the 30 boys he gave Benzedrine had what he described as a "spectacular improvement in school performance". Despite this initial promise, it wasn't until the late 1950's that the use of stimulants became an accepted treatment for hyperactivity in children. As the decades passed, the technology for the delivery of the medication has changed, but the basic principles have more or less stayed the same.

Modern treatment for ADHD still relies on the use of stimulant medication like Ritalin or Adderall because nearly every other therapy has been proven to be useless.

Non-drug treatments for ADHD

There are only two exceptions to that rule. The first is exercise, which seems to have a moderate benefit, and the more exercise the better the outcome.[179] Supplementation with polyunsaturated fatty acids (omega-3 and omega-6 fatty acids) also has an effect, but the effect is tiny.[180]

Ineffective 'treatments'

Other 'treatments' have been shown to be wholly ineffective, including:

- Elimination diets (including those for 'antigenic' foods, specific provoking foods, general elimination diets and 'oligoantigenic' diets)

- Food colouring elimination (including certified food colours, Feingold diets and tartarazine)

- Cognitive training (including working memory specific, and attention specific training)

- Neurofeedback, and

- Behavioural intervention[180]

Ritalin, on the other hand, has been shown to have a strong positive effect on the core symptoms of ADHD. Unfortunately, the research studies themselves have been low quality, causing some people to question the overall outcome of the research.[181]

However, even if the effect of stimulants has been overstated, there's still enough evidence to back the effectiveness of stimulants like Ritalin for children with ADHD compared to other 'treatments', or simply doing nothing and waiting for them to grow out of it (if they ever do).

ADHD Across the Lifespan

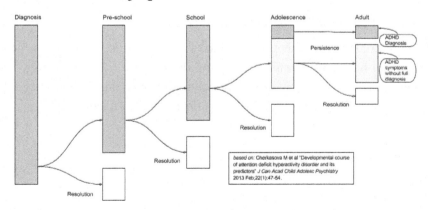

As children with ADHD grow, a proportion of them will have resolution of their symptoms, although some will continue to have symptoms into adulthood

What are the outcomes for children with ADHD?

So what happens when children with ADHD grow up? A number of children with ADHD will fully 'grow out' of their symptoms, that is, they'll have resolution of the illness. They'll become normal adults with a normal attention span and a good chance of a successful life. Their brain has reached maturity, even though it took a little longer to get there.

Unfortunately, ADHD won't fully resolve for most children with it. They'll usually improve to a point as the brain's important circuitry eventually matures to a certain level, and they learn better ways of coping with the residual symptoms.

Residual impairment is still really important though. Adults with lingering symptoms of ADHD have an increased risk of disadvantage. They're more likely to experience poor academic achievement through

ADHD Outcomes into Adulthood

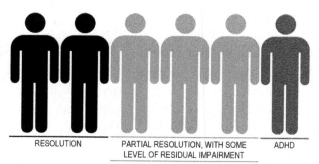

RESOLUTION | PARTIAL RESOLUTION, WITH SOME LEVEL OF RESIDUAL IMPAIRMENT | ADHD

> Poorer academic achievement
> Reduced occupational rank and job performance
> Risky sexual practices
> Early unwanted pregnancies
> Relationship and marital problems
> Traffic violations and car accidents
> Other psychiatric illnesses

Chernissova M, Sutis EM, Dalena RL, Pandic MP, Hechtman L. Developmental course of attention deficit hyperactivity disorder and its predictors. J Can Acad Child Adolesc Psychiatry 2013 Feb;22(1):47-54.

Some children with ADHD will continue to have symptoms into adulthood lower college or university results. They perform poorly within their jobs if they can find a job in the first place. They're more likely to have riskier sex, unwanted pregnancies, and marriage problems. They tend to get more traffic tickets and have more car accidents from riskier driving. They're more likely to develop other mental health problems.

Of course, this doesn't mean they should give up. The majority of adults with residual ADHD can still lead meaningful and productive lives. Some adults will require medication to be able to make it through college or an apprenticeship. Adults with ADHD traits also need to be aware of their own limitations and plan accordingly. For example, they may do their important work at the time of the day they can concentrate best. They may need to schedule regular breaks, or make sure they have enough time to complete tasks, and remember not to take too many tasks on at once. They may be able to use written lists or other visual prompts to keep themselves on track.

And more importantly, we shouldn't give up on them. Understanding and realistic expectations are so important. Working with ADHD is not unlike working with a physical limitation. You wouldn't expect a person with an arm in a sling to perform the same as a person with two functional arms, and by the same token, don't expect a person with some residual ADHD symptoms to necessarily be as productive as anyone else. Having said that, with good management systems in place, the effects of the residual attention issues can minimised, and an otherwise intelligent young adult with residual ADHD can still be highly valuable to any organisation.

Conclusion

ADHD is a very common mental health issue for children.

ADHD is not the result of bad parenting or incorrect discipline, or giving kids too much junk food with sugar and food colouring. ADHD is caused by a large number of genes that each have a small effect. Triggering factors like smoking in pregnancy or severe early childhood trauma cause the nerve cells within the frontal and deep areas like the striatum to grow more slowly and make poorer connections.

For the child, their brain is unable to plan properly, unable to sort through the steps it needs to do something, and unable to control the steps when they're there. As a result, they act on their initial thoughts without understanding the consequences. This leads to the impulsive hyperactivity that can be very disruptive to home and classrooms.

Being unable to pay attention or concentrate on incoming information also makes it very difficult for a child with ADHD to store their information into their memory systems, which adds another impediment to their learning.

ADHD often carries through to adulthood, where various levels of impairment often persist. Adults with ADHD are disadvantaged in all fields of life from studying and working, increased relationship problems, traffic tickets and crashes, and more psychiatric illness.

But it's not all doom and gloom. The medications for ADHD work well and are the most effective treatments available, so that kids can at least have a relatively normal childhood until their brain catches up.

What's more important for most children with ADHD is that they're not stigmatised or criticised for behaviour they find difficult or impossible to control by armchair experts who don't actually know what they're talking about.

14

Autism Spectrum Disorder

Meet James.

James was bright and bubbly. His parents loved him, and so did their camera. Photos of him took prime position on the walls at home, pride of place on work desks, a sizeable chunk of hard drive space, and more than his fair share of Facebook posts.

It was probably the mesmerising effect of his blonde curls, azure-blue eyes, long lashes and cheeky four-toothed smile. The passage of time increased the number of teeth, but not the enchanting impish grin.

When he was around two, James started to scream a lot—a piercing high-pitched scream that started off as a sign of delight, but when he was three, it started to be used as a defence mechanism, employed when another child would try and take something off him or get in his way at child-care.

He also took him longer to talk than the other children. While some of the kids around him in the nursery and the mothers group were talking in sentences, James was sparing with his single words.

As he grew, his parents found that he loved routines. Monday and Wednesday were playgroup days, Tuesdays was the nursery at the ladies meeting at church, grocery shopping on Thursdays, and Fridays were grandparent's day. Every Sunday morning, he went to the nursery at the weekly church celebration. Every afternoon there was lunch, nap, play, and dinner. Sudden changes of plan, like appointments at the doctors, or if his grandparents were sick, or if crèche wasn't available that day, were met with that high pitched scream as well as tears and flailing limbs.

When he was in unfamiliar places or if there was high pitched white noise like hair dryers, James would withdraw or comfort himself by cuddling a soft wool blanket, affectionately called "blankie". If blankie wasn't with him, he would have more screaming and meltdowns.

He also became obsessed with Thomas the Tank Engine. Thomas became part of his daily routine, watching the same four or five episodes every morning for as long as his parents would let him. When he was playing, his Thomas toys would be his first choice. He loved how they stuck together with the little magnets at their ends. He would often turn the trains upside down and spin their wheels for hours by flicking them over and over again with his fingers. He found a particular way of storing them on his bedroom window sill, and would line up his trains in a special order that couldn't be touched or rearranged by anyone without more meltdowns.

When he grew old enough for school, James excelled in anything mathematical. He counted to one hundred by the end of the first term and could recognise complex shapes and patterns. His cooperative play and group activities were the complete opposite. He generally kept to himself in the playground. At the first parent-teacher interview, the teacher suggested to James' parents that a review by a paediatrician might be helpful.

Eventually, James was diagnosed as having autism.

Death by a thousand insults

Over the last few centuries, autism has gone from being considered a form of madness[31] to being popularised on TV (think of "The Big Bang Theory"). 'High functioning' autism, also called Asperger's Syndrome in the old terminology, doesn't make a person look that much different on the outside, but it makes their behaviour somewhat odd to everyone else. They have quirks. They have strange mannerisms. They have rigid ways of doing things. They have very narrow interests. They misread social cues.

"Normal" people, and especially children, don't like odd. Their intolerant tormenting of anyone that doesn't conform to their peer group standards can be merciless and unrelenting. Adults with autism can also be marginalised by their peers, with every barb, joke and isolating experience eroding the soul of the autistic person until eventually there's nothing left. It's death by a thousand insults.

The history of autism

It wasn't until 1943 that autism became widely known in the scientific community. Leo Kanner, a child psychiatrist at Johns Hopkins University School of Medicine in Baltimore, documented eleven children who, while having different presentations, all shared similar traits. They all showed an inability to relate to people, as well as poor speech or unusual use of language, strange responses to objects and events, and an obsession with repetition and sameness, although they also demonstrated excellent rote memory.[182]

Kanner labelled the disorder 'infantile autism'. He thought the condition was a form of psychosis in the same family of disorders as schizophrenia, although separate to schizophrenia itself.[31] He also observed a cold, distant or anti-social nature of the parent's relationship towards the child or the other parent. He thought this may have contributed,[182] and the link with schizophrenia and the concept of "refrigerator mothers" took hold in professional and lay communities alike.

Unbeknown to the rest of the scientific community, a German paediatrician called Hans Asperger had already discovered the same pattern of behaviours in children prior to 1938.[183] Asperger wrote an article for a German language medical journal in 1944, in which he described four highly intelligent boys who all had some aggressive tendencies, a high pitched voice, adult-like choice of words, clumsiness, irritated response to affection, vacant gaze, verbal oddities, prodigious ability with arithmetic and abrupt mood swings. Asperger was the first to propose that these traits were the extreme variant of male intelligence.[184]

Sadly, the full impact of Asperger's discoveries wasn't felt for another half a century until 1981, when British psychiatrist Lorna Wing translated Asperger's original paper into English. By this time, Kanner's version of autism had become a disorder of its own according to the DSM-III, the gold-standard reference of psychiatric diagnosis, but it was still largely defined by the trait of profound deficit. Asperger's description of a 'high-functioning' form of autism resonated amongst the autism community, and a diagnosis of Asperger Syndrome became formally recognised in 1994 with the publication of the DSM-IV.

Because Kanner sold his story first, the view of autism in the 1950s, 60s and 70s was of autism's profound deficit and possible link to schizophrenia. Treatments for autism focused on electric shock, behavioural change techniques involving pain and punishment, and experimental medications such as LSD. It was only during the 1980s and 90s, after Asperger's discoveries and successes came to light, that autism treatment shifted away from the cruel and unusual extremes towards behavioural therapy and the use of highly controlled learning environments.[32]

In 2013, the diagnosis of autism was again revised with the publication of the new version of the DSM, the DSM-5. For the first time, rather than two separate diagnoses, Autism and Asperger's have been linked together as a spectrum and collectively known as Autism Spectrum Disorder (although autism self-advocates prefer the term 'condition' to 'disorder').

How common is autism?

The currently accepted prevalence of ASD (the number of the people in the population that have a diagnosis) is estimated by the Centre for Disease Control in the USA as 1 in 88 (1.13%)[185] although some estimates have been as high as 2.64%, or 1 person in every 38 if screening is done rigorously.[186]

What characterizes autism?

The autism spectrum is defined by two main characteristics: (1) deficits in social and emotional communication and interaction, and (2) restricted repetitive patterns of behaviour.

Social and emotional communication refers to the information that people share with each other about themselves, usually through body language and non-verbal language. Non-verbal language is the tone and rhythm of our speech that people use to communicate information along with the words they speak. A good example of this is sarcasm. Body language also communicates without words, but through our facial expressions, our posture and our body movements. As a basic example, when someone is sad, they can have a drooping posture, leaning forward, looking down, hunched over, with the corners of their mouth being pulled towards the ground.

People on the autism spectrum find social and emotional cues difficult or impossible to interpret. For example, most people understand when another person is being sarcastic, but people on the autism spectrum don't pick up sarcasm that well, and are likely to take the sarcastic comment literally. Sarcastically saying, "Yeah, I really like Gospel Yodelling" to a workmate with ASD will likely land you with the "Best of Gospel Yodelling" CD in your Secret Santa stocking. Or they fail to understand that the furrowing of your forehead and the snarl pulled tightly across your mouth is a sign that they're really annoying you.

The other defining characteristic of the autism spectrum is restricted repetitive patterns of behaviour. This varies from person to person with autism but they have in common a tendency to have extremely strong routines or preferences.

Variety is the spice of life, and people with ASD don't like spicy. For example, people on the autism spectrum may have an overwhelming interest in something specific. For young children, this is often dinosaurs or trains, which then changes as they get older to obsessions with Lego, Minecraft, or something specific to science, like insects, animals, physics or space exploration. While the subject of the obsession is often more mature for adults on the autism spectrum, the difference between a hobby and the obsessional characteristics of the autism spectrum is seen in the amount of time and the singularity with which its pursued.

People on the autism spectrum will also stick to specific routines or rituals, such as always going to work or the shops the same way, every time. People on the autism spectrum will also often repeat the same movements. This is known as stimming. Temple Grandin, a well known author living on the autism spectrum, wrote this about stimming:

"Most kids with autism do these repetitive behaviors because it feels good in some way. It may counteract an overwhelming sensory environment, or alleviate the high levels of internal anxiety these kids typically feel every day. Individuals with autism exhibit a variety of stims; they may rock, flap, spin themselves or items such as coins, pace, hit themselves, or repeat words over and over (verbal stims)."

Children with ASD will often stim in visible ways. Most adults with ASD still stim, but in ways that are less obvious or more socially acceptable, such as wriggling their toes when they're sitting at a desk, out of the view of other people, or unobtrusively rub a part of their clothes or a coin in their pocket.

People on the autism spectrum also tend to have abnormal sensitivity to stimuli. That is, they find certain sounds, smells, or feelings on their skin to be overwhelming and unpleasant, something a neurotypical person would just ignore. For example, people on the spectrum find high pitched white noise like vacuum cleaners or hair dryers distressing, or the feeling of certain fabrics or clothes labels on their skin, or the textures of certain foods in their mouth.

What causes autism?

ASD is recognized as a pervasive developmental disorder. In other words, the effects on development are widespread, affecting a number of developmental pathways. These changes in development result from structural and functional changes in the brain that occur in the womb, and can be detected as early as a month after birth.[53]

Brain changes

In the unborn baby that will be affected by autism, some parts of the brain (mainly the occipital lobes, which deal with vision, and the parietal lobes which process numbers and mathematical problems[187]) have robust nerve cells with a strong synaptic scaffolding, whereas other parts of the brain (especially the frontal lobes and the temporal lobes) will have excess numbers of inefficient nerve cells that are unable to form the correct synaptic scaffolding. So the typical autistic brain is large but out-of-sync.[46, 47]

As I discussed in chapter 4, the reduced scaffolding leads to *local over-connectivity* within regions of the brain, and *under-connectivity between* the regions of the brain.[35]

Remember the city roads example? A normal city has lots of small roads connecting the houses in a suburb, and much larger roads connecting the suburbs. Now imagine a city that had the opposite – arterial roads and freeways between the houses in each suburb, and narrow two lanes roads between the suburbs. You could move really quickly and easily from house to house, but it would be really hard to drive from suburb to suburb. That's what the autistic brain is like.

Because the scaffolding in the vision and mathematics parts of the autistic brain is so dense, it's not a surprise to learn that people on the autism spectrum are very good at visual pattern recognition and mathematical problem solving. Similarly, because the majority of the abnormal connections are within the temporal and frontal lobes of the brain, it's no surprise that by and large, people on the spectrum aren't great with language processing and social cues.[48, 49]

In addition, the cerebellum is significantly linked to the autism spectrum.[50] The cerebellum is the small brain on the back of the big brain and is responsible for fine motor coordination as well as cognition. There's also evidence that the amygdala and hippocampus, involved in controlling emotion and forming certain types of memory, are significantly affected in ASD.[35]

The immune system is also over-active in an autistic person compared to a neurotypical person.[51] These immune changes contribute to the reduced ability of the brain to form new branches as well as develop new nerve cells or remove unnecessary cells (and may contribute to an increased tendency of atopic conditions such as asthma, hay fever, dermatitis, allergies in people on the autism spectrum).

The point of all this is simply to serve as a reminder that the effects of autism are seen in nearly every lobe within the brain.

Genes

The genetic influence on autism is very strong. Twin studies suggest that between 70-90% of the risk of autism is genetic.[33, 34] There are thought to be more than one hundred genes that aren't properly expressed (some are expressed too much, some not enough)[35, 36] The resulting proteins from the abnormal gene expression contribute to a different function of the cell's machinery, altering the ability of a nerve cell to fully develop, and the ability of nerve cells to form connections with other nerve cells.[45]

Environment

There are a number of possible environmental factors that may influence those genes. These include disorders of folate metabolism,[37, 38] pollutants,[39] fever during pregnancy[40] and medications such as valproate and certain anti-depressants[41, 42] which are linked with an increased risk of in autism. Supplements such as folate,[37, 43] omega-6 polyunsaturated fatty acids[44] and the use of paracetamol for fevers in pregnancy[40] have protective effects.

Vaccinations

One final thing to say …

Autism is NOT caused by childhood vaccines.

There's lots of independent science that categorically refutes the claims of anti-vaxxers who still hang onto this idea that the MMR and autism are linked. For example, as stated earlier, the risks for autism are set before birth. Then there's the Cochrane review done by Demicheli and colleagues. Cochrane reviews are the gold standard of independent medical research, and the review by Demicheli et al. looked at the complications associated with the MMR vaccine in more than *one million children*, and found NO ASSOCIATION between MMR and autism. [188]

One more time for good measure: VACCINES DO NOT CAUSE AUTISM. PERIOD.

How is autism managed?

Unlike the conditions that I've outlined in the previous chapters, there is no "cure" for autism.

I know that doesn't sound very hopeful, but it's important to say at the very beginning, because every year there are lots of charlatans, pretend doctors and 'natural healers' that con thousands of desperate parents out of their hard earned money. They prey on the natural instinct of a parent to do all they can for their child. The 'treatments' aren't just useless but so often they're painful or down-right dangerous and can make things worse.

So when you hear anyone tell you that there's a miraculous or sure-fire 'cure' for autism … be it brain training software, a herbal supplement, or some vile old recipe doing the rounds of social media … close your ears and close your wallet. Don't throw good money after bad chasing various brands of snake oil.

Early Intervention

While there may not be a cure for autism, early intervention with intensive therapy can improve IQ and adaptive behaviour in most children.[189] Because there's so much variation in the symptoms and the severity of each child with autism, each therapeutic approach has to be tailored to each child's needs. Obviously what works for an Aspie child with some difficulties within the school social group isn't probably going to work for a non-verbal autistic teenager who tries to rip the carpet off the floor of the doctor's office with his teeth.

Realistic expectations should always accompany therapy. Therapy is unlikely to 'normalise' anyone other than the mildest of Aspies—improvement is more realistic. The aim is to improve the functioning of the child in their environment, to give them as many skills as possible to navigate their social environment as best as they can on their own. Some will do well at school with minimal support. Some will need intensive support at school. Most people on the milder end of the autism spectrum will be able to go to University or find a job, but some will need sheltered workshops.

Medications

Medications only have a small role with autism. Currently there's no drug that improves autism specific symptoms, although some psychiatrists or paediatricians will sparingly use medications to calm down those on the more severe end of the spectrum so they're not a danger to themselves or others. Depression and anxiety often go hand in hand with ASD, and sometimes anti-depressants are required to help with that too.

Acceptance

What people on the autism spectrum really need is acceptance. Most people on the autism spectrum are odd compared to the neurotypical population. They're awkward in social situations. They usually don't get the subtle social signals that other people get naturally, and can make gaffs because they misinterpret what people mean or they're not sure exactly how to behave. They start talking about their particular obsession in the middle of a conversation and then shut down again. Being friends with people on the spectrum can be hard work.

But people on the spectrum have a lot of good qualities. Once you can communicate with them, they're incredibly loyal friends. They find lying difficult so they tend to be honest to a fault. They can often see patterns in things that others can't see.

Take the time to include those people with ASD in your social groups. It will be worth your while.

Autism in the church

One last thing. There are many different types of children's programs ("Sunday schools") just like there are many different styles of churches. Organisers of children's programs need to remember that there are also different types of kids that need to hear the love of God. Kids on the spectrum often don't do well in crowds, or with loud music, or boisterous games. Often they'd prefer to hive off from the main group and go somewhere quiet and play with Legos, or something on an iPad.

Traditionally, those sort of kids have been pushed back into the noisy controlled chaos with the rest of the other kids. Some cope but hide their anxiety, while others feel distressed and will actively avoid children's programs in the future. I would encourage kid's church leaders, where possible, to try and incorporate a separate area for the kids who need a quieter space to be themselves. Use different tools like Legos, or iPad activities—or wherever they're at—to engage those children and teach them the gospel of Jesus in a way that's appropriate to them.

Kids church leaders, please hear my heart: I understand that most of the time it's a stretch just to keep the kids program going every week. What I'm saying here isn't to judge your performance or your heart, or to try and guilt you into adding another complication onto your already busy Sunday morning schedule—you deserve high praise for the investment that you make into the lives of our future generations. I say this because the Great Commission instructs us to go into all the world and preach the gospel, and children on the autism spectrum are a largely untapped people group that process information in a different way, but are still hungry for who Jesus is and what he has to say. Whenever you can, share the gospel in ASD-friendly terms, and create environments that allow kids on the spectrum to participate in their own way. I believe God will reward the effort that you sow with a bountiful harvest.

Conclusion

Autism Spectrum Disorder is a largely genetic disorder that changes the way the brain processes social and emotional signals. There's a broad spectrum of effects that this can have, from the mildest case in which a person wouldn't usually be aware of having the condition, all the way through to the severest forms involving profound behavioural disturbances and intellectual impairment.

There's no cure for autism spectrum disorders, but early intervention shows benefit in improving the symptoms of the condition, and with support and understanding, most people with ASD will learn ways to cope with the condition and function within society.

15

Suicide

Out of all the chapters in the book, this one has been the hardest to write.

Suicide is a difficult subject to discuss. Most people in our Western culture find it difficult to talk about death, and suicide has an extra layer of taboo.

Talking about suicide is uncomfortable, painful, and sometimes downright distressing. Talking about suicide may bring up feelings of grief or loss, or painful memories of when someone we've known died by suicide, or it may remind us of thoughts of suicide we may have once entertained during times of darkness in our life. It may evoke strong feelings through a sense of empathy and compassion with those who have tried it, or succeeded.

Suicide is the act of deliberately killing oneself. Suicide is the major cause of premature death among people with a mental illness and it's estimated that up to one in ten people affected by mental illness die by suicide. Up to 87% of people who die by suicide suffer from mental illnesses. There are more deaths by suicide than deaths caused by skin cancer and car accidents.

Studies in my home country of Australia suggest that about 3% of the population have attempted suicide at some time in their lives. When I first heard that statistic, I had no idea that the number was so high. It's a very telling statistic, and very sad at the same time. Death by suicide costs the economy billions of dollars every year.

While the economic cost of suicide is heavy, the human costs of suicide is far higher. Suicide causes after-shocks which rapidly spread to affect families, workplaces and church communities. The impact of a suicide attempt on first responders, such as police, ambulance and fire brigade, should also not be underestimated. It's estimated that for every suicide, at least six other people are directly impacted in a significant way.[190]

These after-shocks are experienced as the churning tidal swell of grief and loss as well as the crushing distress of unfair self-blame, expressed through questions such as, "Why couldn't I see the warning signs", or "What could I have done or said to prevent the tragedy". The grief, remorse and guilt of family and friends can lead to loss of confidence or self-esteem, or an extra strain on their own network of friends who may not understand their grief or even assist them in coping. The combination of grief, guilt and remorse for family and friends of suicide victims can remain for years.

The weight of the community stigma surrounding suicide also sits heavily on the victim's loved ones. The stigma of suicide is fuelled by those who sit in moral judgment and assume that the act of suicide somehow reflected a personal failure ... the person who took their own life was weak and unable to cope, or the family should have done better and intervened to prevent the suicide. This feeling is particularly strong when the person who took their own life had been known to have a mental illness already.

The stigma towards suicide adds a twist to the already difficult and emotionally draining process of grief, as well as the recovery process for suicide attempt survivors. Stigma fosters further isolation, which in turn increases the risk of financial problems, unemployment, hopelessness and, sadly, an increased future suicide attempts.[191] Bereaved families also face particular dilemmas, such as what to tell others, and the intrusions by police and legal processes surrounding 'sudden death'.

Suicide is a problem that can't be ignored. It might be palpably uncomfortable to discuss, but we can't dismiss it either. It's not only the tragedy of the suicide itself but the darkness and suffering of the resulting fallout that needs to be understood by the church, so that God's light and God's love can be properly demonstrated to those who need it most.

Why do people commit suicide?

It's a very common question when confronted with the topic of suicide. It's a struggle for people to understand how a person could take their own life, and while researchers in the field of mental health understand some of the contributing factors to suicide, there's still a lot more to learn. What is known is that the reasons for suicide are complex and intertwined.

But when you break it all down, suicide is the ultimate expression of hopelessness and helplessness. When a person feels like there's nothing left for them, with no way out, and no one to help, suicide seems like their only option.

There are a number of risk factors known to predispose people to suicidal behaviour. Certain groups of people are more likely to commit suicide: Men, Indigenous people, those experiencing family violence, people who abuse alcohol or drugs, people who are socially or geographically isolated, and those who are grieving. There are also certain warning signs that a particular person may be at risk of suicide: They feel hopeless, they feel trapped, they lack purpose, they withdraw from friends and family, they use more alcohol or drugs, or they may start to deliberately harm themselves.

Risk Factors and Protective Factors for Suicide

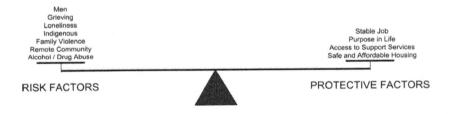

There are also a number of protective factors that can contribute to cushion the risk factors, and help to reduce suicidal behaviour. These include safe and affordable housing, a stable job, access to support services, and the sense of having a purpose to life.

The balance of these risk factors and protective factors influence the overall risk of suicide for a person. If a person's life is heavy with suicide risk factors and light on protective factors, then they're more likely to successfully complete a suicide attempt. Suicide is unlikely if the balance is the other way around.

What's difficult with suicide is that we know about these things in generalities, but it's more difficult to apply these with any certainty in individual people. Some people are able to hide some of the risk factors or their thoughts or plans of suicide from even the best therapist, or closest friends and family. And sometimes, the balance between the risk and protective factors can swing rapidly.

Please understanding that these risk and protective factors are not a precise way of predicting who will and who won't try suicide. They're also not a tool to beat yourself up with if you know someone close to you who tried to, or successfully committed suicide. It's not a case of, "I should have picked up on these risk factors." I'm explaining these risk and protective factors to help people understand more about suicide, not to become a suicide-gnostic. As I said before, sometimes people can successfully hide their suicidal thoughts from their closest friends and family, or deny them, or lie about them. We all do our best to prevent suicides. If a person succeeds in their suicide attempt, it's normal to look for something or someone to blame, but the 'what if's' don't help.

Signs of imminent risk

There are, however, signs of imminent risk—behaviours and characteristics that are commonly seen in people just before they attempt suicide. Again, I can't stress enough, not everyone shows these signs, but according to research, many people who are seriously considering suicide tell someone about their suicidal thoughts or plans either through their words or actions.

If someone:

- is threatening to hurt or kill themselves or expressing an intent to die

- is looking at ways to attempt suicide, or talking about their suicide plan

- has access to lethal means (e.g., firearms, rope, cars, sharp knives or razor blades)

- is displaying impulsive, aggressive, or anti-social behaviour, particularly when it's unusual or out-of-character for the person, or the person is displaying a sense of urgency or crisis

- has a sudden change in mood to seemingly calm and peaceful (this is often after the person has made a decision to end their life)

...then please seek professional advice.

Sometimes suicides can be prevented by removing access to lethal means (removing knives or razor blades, or taking their car keys for a while), but sometimes an urgent review with a mental health professional is required, or an admission to hospital. Don't ever hesitate to get professional help when you think someone may be at imminent risk of suicide.

Preventing suicides

Suicide is a problem with many layers, and preventing suicide needs to be just as layered. Suicide prevention is as much a community and government issue as it is an individual issue.

Reduce lethal means

One of the most important ways to tackle suicide as a community is by reducing access to lethal means of suicide. In Australia, the tough gun laws introduced in the 1990's helped reduce the number of suicides, and it's estimated that restriction of access to barbiturate medications in the 1960's reduced the suicide rate by over 20%.

Gatekeeper training

Another broad systematic strategy is called Gatekeeper training. Gatekeepers include frontline workers in formal helping roles directly associated with health, safety and wellbeing, and those whose public contact roles place them in a position to notice when someone may be at risk. This includes the usual health and helping professionals like psychologists, paramedics, police officers, nurses and doctors, as well as pastors, church small group leaders, teachers, chaplains, or coaches.

Community wide strategies

A study in 2003 showed that a community-wide suicide prevention strategy reduced the suicide rate within the US air force community by 33% over a six-year period.[192] Different training is needed for groups with different community responsibility and access. Increasing awareness and decreasing stigma through initiatives like "R U Ok" are good for the population level, but those in formal helping roles such as welfare workers, crisis support workers, counsellors and trained pastors, would be trained in more formal suicide prevention skills as part of their training.

Appropriate medications

As we've discussed elsewhere in the book, psychiatric medications are useful treatments for those suffering from anxiety, depression, schizophrenia, and other mental health problems. As noted by Correll and colleagues, "clozapine, antidepressants, and lithium, as well as anti-epileptics, are associated with reduced mortality from suicide. Thus, the potential risks of antipsychotics, antidepressants and mood stabilizers need to be weighed against the risk of the psychiatric disorders for which they are used and the lasting potential benefits that these medications can produce."[193]

Anti-depressants and other psychiatric medications aren't side-effect free, and their effectiveness is limited. Neither can they address the variety of psychological and social factors that contribute to someone's risk of suicide. As such, we need to have realistic expectations of them, but since they're beneficial more often than not, they shouldn't be discouraged.

Psychological therapies

There is also supportive evidence for good psychological treatment care, including CBT (which we've discussed in previous chapters), as well as dialectical behaviour therapy, family therapy, and problem-solving therapy. Psychological treatments such as these have been shown to be directly effective in reducing suicidal thoughts and behaviours.

Collaborative care models

Collaborative care involves multiple tools and strategies for managing depression in a primary care practice population. These interventions include education and decision support for primary care clinicians, along with use of "depression care managers" who are often specially trained primary care nurses. Care managers continuously monitor patient outcomes, provide patient education, encourage and monitor treatment adherence, and facilitate communication among patients, their primary care physicians, and mental health clinicians. Meta-analyses have shown collaborative care for depression to be both more effective and, at larger population levels, more cost-effective than treatment as usual.[194]

Others

There are many other ways in which suicide can be reduced. Media coverage of suicides can sometimes promote the idea of suicide to others, but responsible media reporting of deaths by suicide helps to reduce this accidental promotion. Suicide is also reduced through funding to services such as crisis telephone lines and services, front line staff in psychiatric facilities, and counselling for loved ones of those who have lost someone to suicide.

Going into full details on each of these strategies would need a book by itself, but there is one more critical thing to discuss, something that the Christian church is built for.

Connection

Genuine connection within a supportive, caring social environment is protective against suicide. Supportive, caring social environments are what churches are all about – it's in church DNA! The early church provides the blueprint of the model church, which according to Acts 2:42, "They were devoting themselves to the apostles' teaching and to fellowship, to the breaking of bread and to prayer." The early church did this because of love – love for God that invariably spilled over into love for each other.

Every church is different, a unique synergy of people with characteristics of the community that flows through them. This natural variation makes it hard to give blanket advice as to exactly how each church community can foster genuine connection with those people who are not always the most lovable, or who are not able to give a lot of love in return. The core principles of the early church – they loved God and therefore they loved each other, provide the most fundamental instruction. The gospel of Jesus was a priority, as were times of prayer together, but they also hung together – they fellowshipped in ministry together, they ate together, and they celebrated life together. They accepted each other and provided a safe place for their members to share their problems in safety, because they knew they wouldn't be criticized or harshly judged.

This is a good place to start from. Love God with all your heart, soul, mind and strength, and allow God's love to flow through you to those around you. Build a true community of connection through acceptance and fellowship.

It's easy to hang out with people you like, and are like you. It's not as fun when you have a damp squid tagging along, or someone who's highly strung, or who has occasional manners and no social skills. Except that for the person who is the damp squid/highly strung/no-social-sense, hanging out with people and having normal human connection can be as good as therapy.

The power of one ...

When I was a teenager, I went through a very difficult time. I had a very serious case of social anxiety disorder, and it was debilitating. I had a couple of friends at school, and other than my family, they were the only people I felt comfortable speaking to. Speaking to anyone else would fill me with varying levels of dread. I could cope with crowds only if I didn't have to speak to anyone, and I could hide from the public view, but being forced to go on camps or to youth group would fill me with paralysing anxiety that would take me days to get over.

I started to improve when I had a change of church. When I was about to enter my senior year of high school, my family moved to a new church whose youth group was welcoming and supportive. They accepted me despite my painfully shy exterior. They encouraged me to join in with activities, but gave me space if I needed it. They treated me as one of the gang, as an equal. One of the youth leaders ran the drama group, and I joined it just to be polite and help her out with numbers, but over time I went from an extra to having major roles. Learning to perform boosted my self-confidence and I learnt social skills by being around normal people and copying what they did.

To this day, I'm very grateful for those guys who welcomed me, accepted me, and who helped me grow. Their kindness changed the course of my life. I'm sure it wasn't easy for them. In fact, one youth leader, Liza, literally went above and beyond. She was my transport just about everywhere for about four years for all youth social events.

Their acceptance came at a time in my life when I was at a crossroads. If I hadn't stayed in church, I doubt I would have been able to finish school and get my degree. Their sacrifice and support made a profound difference in my life.

Sometimes you don't have to plant churches or preach from a street corner or evangelize an unreached people group in a jungle somewhere to change the course of history. Sometimes all you need to do is welcome that awkward, fumbling anxious kid into your social sphere and treat them as an equal. Sometimes a kind word and a helping hand are more powerful than a crusade or concert. "The King will reply, 'Truly I tell you, whatever you did for one of the least of these brothers and sisters of mine, you did for me.'"

Conclusion

Suicide is a hidden plague that affects our society, and the church is not immune. The reasons why someone might attempt or commit suicide are complex and intertwined, but simply put, suicide is the ultimate expression of hopelessness and helplessness. When a person feels like there's nothing left for them, with no way out, and no one to help, suicide seems like their only option.

There are a number of ways in which suicide can be reduced or prevented, some of which are at community and government levels, but there are also ways in which individuals can reduce the risk of suicide in their community and promote protective factors. These can range from simply increasing awareness and decreasing stigma about mental health problems as well as increasing training in suicide intervention for those in formal helping roles such as welfare workers, crisis support workers, counsellors and trained pastors. One of the ways that the Christian community can help in suicide prevention is to simply build networks of genuine connection within a supportive, caring social environment for those Christians who struggle with mental health problems or social connection and relationships.

16

Enhancing recovery

From the beginning of the book, we've looked at mental health and illness from a number of different perspectives. We've looked at the way the brain works, how our brains make thoughts and what our thoughts and feelings really mean. We've looked at how we process stress, and when good stress becomes distress. We've looked at things that promote better mental health, and the causes and treatments of the most common mental illnesses.

This chapter is about living with mental illness, specifically about helping the people that live with mental illness and those who care for them.

It's also for everyone else. Mental illness affects everyone, directly or indirectly, and there are some simple ways that you can support those around you who are touched by the dark affliction of poor mental health.

These tips are meant to work in addition to the treatments we've discussed in previous chapters. They're not a replacement. Successfully living with mental ill-health involves good medical and psychological treatments first and foremost. What I'll discuss in this chapter is more general … tips and thoughts that are in addition to specific treatments like long term therapy with a psychologist, or medications if required.

Living better with mental illness

Accept faith and medicine

As Christians, it's natural to want to live by faith, or to be in the world but not of the world. We have our own Christian jargon, our own music, our own traditions, and even our own B-grade movies and TV programs. So I understand why many Christians only want to have prayer counselling, or to reject medication in favour of faith healing.

I also hear Christians dismiss the so-called 'secular' discipline of psychology as if it's heathen. This attitude is sometimes encouraged by Christian leaders or so-called Christian mental health 'experts'.

Whatever the reason, these Christians refuse treatments that are proven to be helpful for managing mental ill-health because they're deemed to be not 'Christian' enough.

It can also happen the other way. In the midst of the chaos or the darkness, some Christians lose sight of their faith and abandon prayer, the Bible, or the Christian church. Abandoning these pillars of the Christian life further isolates them from their traditions, their community and their deepest beliefs and values.

The solution is to accept both faith and medicine.

As we discussed in the chapter on FACT, we need to accept our thoughts and feelings for what they are and stop fighting them, but we also need to move forward towards our deepest values. For Christians, our deepest values draw from our faith and love for God, who loves us beyond measure and who's always there for us, even when it's too dark for us to see him.

We also need to accept that God sometimes heals through medicine and science as much as he sometimes heals supernaturally. Just like we accept medical help for physical illnesses while we trust God for our healing, accepting help from psychotropic medications or counselling from psychologists can ease the burden of mental illness while we wait on God for full healing in His timing.

God wants the best for us. He gave us brains so that we can use them. We don't stand outside in a storm and pray for God to provide shelter when we can just walk into our house. He gave us brains to build houses. He also gave us brains to make medicines and understand the human psyche. I think it's respectful, and even a form of worship to God, to use medications and counselling so long as we thank God for them.

You're not weak or malingering

There's a surprising number of people in the secular community and in the church that would tell you that mental illnesses aren't real. One prominent speaker, held in high esteem by many in the Christian church, wrote once that depression and ADHD weren't actually diseases, they were just normal human emotions that were deliberately mislabelled by the American Psychiatric Association as a way of making more profit.

It's unfortunate when popular church leaders start teaching such things, because as preposterous as it sounds, people in the church start believing it. After a little while, that's how they start treating people with mental illnesses.

"You're not really depressed, you're just sad. You just need to cheer up. Turn that frown upside down. What, you can't?! Well, you must be just making it up for attention then, because this preacher said that depression isn't really a disease."

After a while, you start believing it yourself.

Don't let someone else's ignorance make things hard for you. Remember, depression or anxiety aren't diseases just because the American

Psychiatric Association declared them to be so. It's not all in your head or a figment of your imagination. You're not putting it on for the fun of it.

Depression, anxiety, schizophrenia, bipolar, ADHD... they're all real diseases with a rational biological basis. And because they have a biological basis, there is often a biologically based treatment. Being labelled with a mental illness doesn't remove all hope – it's just the opposite. A correct diagnosis means that the correct treatment can be given. It's a turning point–there is hope!

The other thing to remember is that having a mental illness is like having a physical illness. When you have a physical illness, you don't function 'normally'. Things are harder. Your body doesn't do what you want it to do.

For example, you might be able to go to work with a bit of a cold, although everything seems more difficult. But what if you had pneumonia, and you were shaking and sweating with high fevers, gasping for breath between chest-crushing fits of coughing? Could you go to work then? Well, again, some people could, but it would be a real challenge. In that state, it would be an unbelievable show of strength for most people just to make it out of bed.

When you have a mental illness, you don't function 'normally'. Things are harder. Your thoughts, feelings and emotions, and sometimes your physical body, doesn't do what you want it to do. Severe mental illness is the the psychological equivalent of having a severe physical illness like pneumonia. People with pneumonia tend to lay in bed and sleep a lot, not because they're lazy, but because their body is working very hard to kill the invading bacteria and heal itself, working at twice the usual metabolic rate but without getting all the oxygen it needs because the lungs are full of pus and goo. For someone with pneumonia, getting out of bed and getting dressed is a feat. Getting out their front door is a miracle.

While it may appear to other people that you're weak because you have a hard time getting to work every day and concentrating on your job, the truth is the exact opposite. Living with mental illness requires enormous inner strength to complete even the most basic tasks, because you have to work ten times harder to make your unwilling brain and psyche do what you need to do. It would be so much easier to stay in bed all day and sleep between bouts of crying, or stay away from the things that cause unimaginable dread. Getting out the door takes enormous inner strength.

So don't let anyone tell you that because you're weak because you have a mental illness. Ignore what the ignorant may tell you. You're much stronger than you think! Give yourself some credit.

You don't lack faith

This is another subtle lie that's an extension of the weak/malingering fallacy. It's another little gem that's said by well-meaning but ignorant preachers and teachers. It goes like this: "God only made good stuff … who messes it up? We do!"

In other words, it's not God's fault you're messed up–it's yours. And if it's your fault, then it must be because of something you've done, or something you're lacking.

So the final conclusion varies between people, but inevitably, people with poor mental health assume that they're the root cause of their own problems. They've sinned, or they lack faith.

"I just need more faith. Then I wouldn't feel this way."

It's the spiritual form of the other incessant, tortuous little thought that keeps buzzing your brain, "I just need to cheer myself up/calm myself down."

In the end, it's a pointless exercise … a form of mental and spiritual self-flagellation. It doesn't help us to go anywhere except down.

I understand that when your brain is bound by a mental illness of some form, it typically doesn't process thoughts that well. If you can, it helps to remember that being physically sick isn't the result of a lack of faith, and it's the same for mental ill-health. Some of the most faithful people that I know have gone through their own period of mental ill-health. There are many triggers to a mental illness, and most of them are beyond our control. Mental illness is not the result of a spiritual failing. Which brings us on to the next point.

You're still worthy of God's love

When you're struggling with anything in life, it's easy to have self-doubt. Struggling with mental illness is even tougher to deal with. The feeling of fighting and fighting, and not getting anywhere … it makes you feel like a failure.

The constant feeling of stagnation can have different effects on different people. Sometimes, it just makes you tired. Sometimes people feel so tired that they feel like giving up. The failure and the frustration often takes a toll on a person's self esteem. You end up thinking you must deserve what you've got, that you're meant to be suffering. Or you must have done something wrong to bring this affliction upon yourself.

Mental illness often changes how you process feelings too, especially love and hope. This makes it hard to enjoy the warmth of love and friendship, from the people around you, and from God himself.

From here, the logical conclusion is that God is so far away, because of something that you've done, so you must be unworthy of God's love.

I've been there, personally. Some of the spiritually darkest times I've had in my life have been when my mental health has been at its worst.

Again, it's not always easy in those dark times, emotionally and spiritually, but don't forget what the Bible says. This is probably one of my favourite all-time passages, because of what it meant to me when I realised the power of the words that Paul wrote:

"Who shall separate us from the love of Christ? Shall trouble or hardship or persecution or famine or nakedness or danger or sword? ... No, in all these things we are more than conquerors through him who loved us. For I am convinced that neither death nor life, neither angels nor demons, neither the present nor the future, nor any powers, neither height nor depth, nor anything else in all creation, will be able to separate us from the love of God that is in Christ Jesus our Lord." (Romans 8:35,37-39)

You may not feel worthy of God's love, but God's love doesn't depend on you, it depends on God. Think of a TV with a broken aerial. The TV's signal doesn't depend on the aerial ... the signal is exactly the same. It's everywhere, all the time, at the same intensity. It just so happens that the TV can't pick up the signal properly. God's love for you is exactly the same. It's everywhere, all the time, at the same intensity. Mental illness makes it hard to understand and accept God's love, but God's love is just the same.

Your value to God doesn't change. If I have two new one hundred dollar bills, fresh from the bank, and I take one and rub it on my armpit, spit on it, and smear it with fertiliser, it still has exactly the same value as the one that's been in my wallet. The intrinsic value of the money doesn't change, even though it's been through some unpleasant experiences. Living with a mental illness may make you feel like you're unlovable, worthless, or of no value. Though to God, your intrinsic value never changes. His grace and love for us never changes. You're as valuable and as worthy of his love as the day he made you.

You're not useless

In the middle of the darkest depression or the paralysis of severe anxiety, it's easy to think that you're no good to anyone. You may feel like you're of no use because you're of no worth.

Thankfully, the promises of God are unchanging, and aren't dependant on our mental state. Just as Paul wrote to the Romans that "nothing shall separate us from the love of God", he also wrote some profound words to the Ephesians:

"For we are God's workmanship, created in Christ Jesus to do good works, which God prepared in advance for us to do." (Ephesians 2:10)

The word "workmanship" is the Greek word *poēma*, which is where we get our English word "poem." We're not a meaningless jumble of letters that make no sense. We're a beautifully crafted blend of rhythm, harmony and meaning. You are a sonnet from the mouth of God. And you were "created ... to do good works". Your life is one of purpose.

The whole "life of purpose" thing has been taught so often in Christian circles in the last couple of decades that it's in danger of become cliché and losing its power, but the power and the promise of God's word doesn't change. You may feel like your mental illness disqualifies you from what God has planned for you. God doesn't.

Mental illness doesn't change your value or your purpose.

If anything, experiencing the brokenness of mental illness and recovery makes your appreciation of God's grace deeper and more profound. Like the kintsukuroi pot, where every crack and blemish is lined with gold, it's because of our brokenness that we are more beautiful and more valued than before.

Helping better with mental illness

For Christians living with mental illness, life can be pretty tough, though it's often made just that little bit harder by the attitudes of others in the church. There are some well-meaning Christians in the church who try to 'help' in ways that are based on their assumptions about mental illness. There are others who feel like they don't know anything about mental illness and avoid helping altogether.

This book is about helping Christians with mental health problems live more productive lives. One way is through education—education of those who suffer with mental illness as well as education of those who don't. Even a small increase in understanding mental illness helps those Christians with good mental health to empathise a little more with Christians who live with mental health problems.

There are some easy things that everyone can do to make life that little bit easier for those Christians struggling with mental illness.

Sensitivity

All people with mental health issues are on a spectrum of severity. Some people are quite functional – they still struggle with their challenging feelings and thoughts, but can still go to work, participate in church activities and go out with friends. Then there are others who are so bound by their symptoms that they can't function at all.

Most sufferers of mental illness are somewhere in between, and can move up or down the spectrum day by day, or sometimes even moment to moment.

This can be hard for those people who live or work with someone with mental illness—one moment they seem relatively happy, the next minute they melt into tears or explode in anger. Or they're just perpetually grumpy and snap at everything, or they're constantly apprehensive. It's hard work to have to put up with the near-constant down-vibe. It strains relationships and dampens the atmosphere.

It's understandable why people would rather avoid the melancholic Dr Jekyll who becomes the cantankerous Mr Hyde ... it's so much easier to be around 'normal' people. Yet one of the biggest stumbling blocks to the recovery of people with mental illness is isolation. Admittedly, sometimes when you're depressed or anxious, you really don't want to be around people, but then there are times, especially as someone recovers, that they'd like to do some everyday stuff with everyday people. Not always lots of stuff ... but just gradually increasing time with regular people in a social setting.

Unfortunately, years of isolation tend to destroy friendships, limit social skills, make people feel awkward, or leave people labelled as that "mentally unstable" guy. These things can make being in a social group uncomfortable for the regular guys and the person in recovery. Sometimes there's also the residual depression or anxiety to make things difficult as well. Failed attempts at reintegration can lead to more isolation.

So if you really want to help someone with a mental illness recover, sensitivity and understanding are important keys:

~ Offer a genuine hand of friendship.

~ Don't be afraid of rejection. Sometimes, people with a mental illness do need space, or aren't ready for regular human interaction. So ...

~ Give the person in recovery as much time as they need, and

~ Keep offering the hand of friendship.

If a person in mental health recovery does accept your offer, be prepared for them to:

~ Change their minds

~ Want to be out for a short time

~ Come out with the group, but be quiet or unassuming

~ Feel or look awkward, or not know what to say, or make a faux pas every now and then.

Be patient. A person recovering from mental illness has to crawl before they can run. They're going to have times when they fall over. Offer them your hand if they fall, but give them space and time if they don't accept straight away.

It may seem like a lot of work, and some people in recovery are genuinely needy. Try not to do everything on your own—work with others. Remember, statistically there are four mentally healthy people on average for every person who is not, so don't just bear the load, share the load. It will make a massive difference to the recovery of a person afflicted with mental illness.

Openness

Along with isolation, one of the biggest obstacles to recovery of a person with a mental illness is stigma, the prejudice and discrimination that face those with mental health problems.

Despite the daily scientific breakthroughs in the why and how of most psychological disorders, those that suffer from mental illness continue to face rejection from their friends, neighbours and workmates.

For example, it's been reported that 47% of people indicated that they would be unwilling to work on a job with someone with depression; 62% expressed unwillingness to work with a person with schizophrenia. One-third indicated a belief that those with major depression were likely to be violent toward others while nearly two-thirds expected violence from someone with schizophrenia.[195]

As a result of these pervasive attitudes, people with mental illness are less likely to be offered a job, be rented an apartment, or be accepted by a university. Naturally, discrimination at this level makes it very difficult for a person with mental illness to lead a normal life, which only adds further obstacles to recovery, like unemployment, poverty and even homelessness.

The isolation and discrimination has a detrimental effect on recovery. Most people with mental illness won't seek a diagnosis or treatment for fear of stigma, and stigma leads to decreased rates of adherence to treatment. They become anxious about who they can share their diagnosis with. Hiding their secret day in and day out causes discomfort, shame and loss of self-esteem and the ongoing stress further erodes their mental and physical health.

As a Christian, you can make an enormous difference by being open to people with mental illness, and by rejecting the social stigma of mental illness.

Making and keeping friends is one of the hardest things for people recovering from mental illness, partly because of their own internal emotional difficulties, but also because of the rejection by others based on the false expectations that make up the stigma surrounding mental illness. As we discussed earlier in the section on sensitivity, simply being a friend can make a major difference to a person on the recovery path.

Though being open to people with a mental illness isn't the only step here. You can also combat stigma by calling it out when you see it. Western society has largely overcome some of it's deepest, centuries-old prejudices, such as sexism and racism. There's no reason why prejudice and discrimination against those with mental illness can't be overcome either. It starts with one voice saying, "Enough!" Each new voice adds to the crescendo until eventually, those who choose to promote fear and prejudice against those with mental illness have no where to hide. Remember, one drop of rain isn't a flood, but millions of drops can become a flood. There's power in numbers. Play your part.

Acceptance of medication and counselling

This seems to be a bit of a no-brainer. Medication and psychological therapy are the mainstay of treatment for mental health problems, but it saddens me to say that there are still mainstream preachers, some of them who are promoted within the church as mental health 'experts', who slander psychiatric medications and sow distrust of modern psychology.

This sort of misguided teaching entrenches ingrained myths and promotes ignorance amongst the body of Christ.

It also makes life very difficult for Christians who are suffering from, or recovering from mental illness. As I've discussed in previous chapters, medications and counselling are proven to offer benefit to patients with mental illness. Collectively, they improve health and well-being, increase life expectancy and reduce the rate of suicide.

Ignorance on the part of well meaning Christians increases the stigma of mental illness and its treatment. Christians with mental illness are told that secular psychologists aren't God-honouring, or that psychiatric medications are poisonous, ineffective, and based on an evolutionary world view. Those that do continue with secular psychology or psychiatric medication are stigmatised for accepting "unbiblical, unchristian" treatments, or are pushed to use 'treatments' that have no proven benefit, or simply accept no treatment at all. Rather than take meaningful steps to recovery, they're left isolated or in free-fall.

Church, it's time to step into the 21ˢt century and move beyond the unscientific presumptions that have plagued the Christian church throughout the ages. Medications and psychological treatments like CBT and ACT are effective therapeutic tools that, when used judiciously, help more people than not.

If you want to help those around you on the road to mental health recovery, encourage them to seek appropriate treatment from qualified professionals. Don't spread myths or hearsay about secular psychology or medications like anti-psychotics or anti-depressants.

Openly question the so-called experts who criticise these treatments. Ask where they got their information from, or why they think it's ethically appropriate to undermine treatments which are beneficial to the majority of patients with mental illness.

If we're seriously going to help people recover from mental illness, we have to encourage effective treatments based on science instead of spreading malicious misinformation based on ignorance and presumption.

Prayer and faith

While we should embrace treatments proven by good science to be effective, we should also embrace the core of our spiritual life, namely prayer and faith. While the evidence for prayer as a treatment modality may not be as scientifically robust as the evidence for CBT or pharmaceuticals, the prayer of faith is a central tenet of our spirituality as Christians. It's something that can be encouraged as part of the toolbox for Christians on the road to psychological recovery.

Always remember to be sensitive to a person's place on the journey, and to their daily struggles that they face. A person recovering from mental illness may not want attention or public prayer (or indeed, *any* prayer). If you feel the prompting of the Holy Spirit to pray for someone, ask permission first. Be sensitive with your language, your tone, your exuberance. Be careful to avoid making assumptions about that person. If they don't want you to pray for them there and then, pray privately, and give them the space they need. Be supportive, not pushy.

When it's done right, prayer for those recovering from mental ill-health can be a lightning rod for the three pillars of our Christianity – faith, hope and love. Prayer connects us to God through faith, it ignites our hope, and it motivates through love. The same goes for all illness, of course, physical and mental, though I think with mental illness in particular, this can truly bring about meaningful change. Mental illness often leaves its sufferers faithless, hopeless and unloved, whereas prayer motivated by the right motivation and powered by the Holy Spirit, restores love and reconnects faith, which in turn stimulates new hope.

So, embrace science, and embrace faith. They're two sides of the same coin. Sensitively use prayer to help people on the road to recovery.

Empathy

I discussed before that isolation and stigma are two significant obstacles on the road to mental health recovery, and what connects stigma and isolation together is shame. Shame is the fear of disconnection, the sense of "If other people saw who I really am, they would reject me." Shame isn't limited to people with mental health problems, but the profound sense of shame shared by people with mental illness often leads to a deeper sense of aloneness and a greater fear of making connections with others.

Brené Brown, an American social worker and researcher who studies shame for a living, said that shame needs three things to thrive: secrecy, silence and judgement. Stigma provides a major disincentive to those with a mental health diagnosis coming out. You're already fighting an illness that has crushed your soul and deprived you of hope. You also see how mental illness is treated by society, and you know you don't need that added burden. The easiest way to avoid the expected judgement and general disdain from those surrounding you is to hide, to deliberately stay silent, to shield your broken soul with a wall of secrecy, but that only feeds the feelings of shame.

Again, as Brené Brown insightfully says, "Empathy is the antidote to shame ... The two most powerful words when we're in struggle are 'me too.'"

According to Psychology Today, "Empathy is the experience of understanding another person's condition from their perspective. You place yourself in their shoes and feel what they are feeling." Empathy is feeling with people.

There are four attributes of empathy:

1. To be able to see the world as others see it

2. To be nonjudgmental

3. To understand another person's feelings

4. To communicate your understanding of that person's feelings

So often we confuse empathy with sympathy. Sympathy is a feeling of care and concern for someone, together with a wish to see that person better off or happier, but sympathy, unlike empathy, does not involve a shared perspective or shared emotions. We understand that the person is in a difficult space, but we see their problem from our perspective, not their perspective. Sympathy is often judgemental and dismissive.

Sympathy often says, "At least ..." or "It could be worse ...".

Like, "At least you've still got a job", or "At least you're still married", or "Well there are other people around the world living in cardboard boxes, so it could be worse."

Empathy says, "I've been there, and that really hurts," or "It sounds like you're in a hard place now. Tell me more about it."

Understanding the perspective of those on the road to mental health recovery helps to nullify the shame of mental illness. Being vulnerable, open and non-judgemental breaks the silence and negates the need for secrecy, which overcomes shame and breaks the link that shame forms between stigma and isolation.

If you want to make the road to recovery smoother for those with mental health problems, understand their perspective without making judgement. Give them the empathy they need.

Conclusion

So to recap, when it comes to living better with mental illness:

- Accept faith and medicine
- You're not weak or malingering
- You don't lack faith
- You're still worthy of God's love
- You're not useless

Mentally strong and healthy people can make a massive difference to the church by helping better with mental illness:

- Sensitivity

- Openness

- Acceptance of medication and counselling

- Prayer and faith

- Empathy

Doing these things will truly help the people that matter, the people that live with mental illness, and it will help them recover and fulfil their potential and their destiny in God.

17

The Most Important Step

"The journey of a thousand miles begins with a single step"
–Lao Tzu

When I wrote this book, I wanted it to speak to as many different people as possible.

Perhaps you're reading this book because you or a loved one are on the road to mental health recovery. Sometimes the road to restoration can seem very long. Redemption seems like the proverbial mirage, always shimmering in the distance, and never getting closer. I know. I've been there.

I've fought many rounds with mental illness over the years, and there were many times on each road to recovery where I thought I could go no further. The going was too tough, and I was too tired.

Even though there were times I didn't think there was any hope or any point, I took the most important step in my journey, which was the 'next' step. Then I took the next. And the next. Each 'next' step brought me closer to completing the journey, every little bit adding up to recovery. That's why I'm still here today.

Some days there were more 'next' steps than others. Some days, there were none. Sometimes those days stretched out to weeks. I know that feeling where everything feels overwhelming and it's much easier to watch TV re-runs with a bottle of wine, or just hide in bed in the dark and pretend the world isn't there, and on those days I could do nothing more than rely on God's grace and love to pull me through.

In this book, I've discussed a lot of different theories about how our brains work and why we experience different forms and degrees of mental illness. I've also discussed a lot of different strategies and treatment options for various conditions. They're all very well and good, but as I discussed in the chapter on FACT, if we want to live a life rich in meaning, we have to do that through committed action. It's God desire that we are not only restored, but also rejuvenated. He can take our brokenness and repair it with gold, but in order to do that, we need to accept his grace by moving with him along the journey. Which brings me to a very important question:

What's your 'next' step?

Maybe you've never suffered from a mental illness but you're reading this book to discover more about mental health and the challenge it presents for the Christian church? I really respect that! Anyone who has struggled with their mental health for any significant length of time will have met the well-meaning but misunderstanding Christian who wants to help but can make things confusing instead. I applaud everyone who wants to understand mental health better, and who advocates for and supports those who struggle with poor mental health.

Still, the same question also applies … what's your 'next' step?

For all of us, whether you've experienced the struggles of mental illness first hand or whether you're searching for more information, the best way to get the most out of this book is to take some committed action. It doesn't have to be big, and it doesn't have to be difficult, but it helps if it's specific.

Perhaps it's accepting that you don't have to fight with your thoughts any more. Perhaps it's taking the time to practice a few minutes of mindfulness. Maybe you can start a gratitude diary. Maybe you can find room to accept God's grace and forgiveness, and to forgive yourself. Maybe you decide to talk to your local doctor about your depression, or get counselling from a psychologist about your anxiety. Maybe you can to get along side someone who's struggling with mental illness in your church and start a conversation. Maybe you can talk about mental health in your home group or cell group meeting.

It may be a little step, and that's ok. The 'next' step is always the most important step.

Once you take that step, then take the next step. And the next step. And the next.

Don't give up. God never gives up on us. Remember, everything that has the capacity to be broken also has the capacity for redemption. Think of the kintsukuroi bowl. God turns things that are broken into things of beauty.

I hope and pray that through this book, you will have a better understanding of mental health and illness, and that together as a church, we would grow stronger together to support those still struggling, so that our gold seams would give them encouragement to take their next step into recovery.

That's how we truly become Kintsukuroi Christians.

References

1 Berns G. Iconoclast : a neuroscientist reveals how to think differently. Boston: Harvard Business School Press, 2008.

2 Epstein R. The neural-cognitive basis of the Jamesian stream of thought. Consciousness and cognition 2000 Dec;9(4):550-75.

3 Repovs G, Baddeley A. The multi-component model of working memory: explorations in experimental cognitive psychology. Neuroscience 2006 Apr 28;139(1):5-21.

4 Baars BJ, Franklin S. How conscious experience and working memory interact. Trends in cognitive sciences 2003 Apr;7(4):166-72.

5 Baars BJ. Global workspace theory of consciousness: toward a cognitive neuroscience of human experience. Progress in brain research 2005;150:45-53.

6 Bor D, Seth AK. Consciousness and the prefrontal parietal network: insights from attention, working memory, and chunking. Frontiers in psychology 2012;3:63.

7 Jolij J, Lamme VA. Repression of unconscious information by conscious processing: evidence from affective blindsight induced by transcranial magnetic stimulation. Proceedings of the National Academy of Sciences of the United States of America 2005 Jul 26;102(30):10747-51.

8 Ohman A, Flykt A, Esteves F. Emotion drives attention: detecting the snake in the grass. Journal of experimental psychology General 2001 Sep;130(3):466-78.

9 Haggard P. Human volition: towards a neuroscience of will. Nature reviews Neuroscience 2008 Dec;9(12):934-46.

10 Libet B, Gleason CA, Wright EW, Pearl DK. Time of conscious intention to act in relation to onset of cerebral activity (readiness-potential). The unconscious initiation of a freely voluntary act. Brain : a journal of neurology 1983 Sep;106 (Pt 3):623-42.

11 Soon CS, Brass M, Heinze HJ, Haynes JD. Unconscious determinants of free decisions in the human brain. Nature neuroscience 2008 May;11(5):543-5.

12 Bonn GB. Re-conceptualizing free will for the 21st century: acting independently with a limited role for consciousness. Frontiers in psychology 2013;4:920.

13 Horga G, Maia TV. Conscious and unconscious processes in cognitive control: a theoretical perspective and a novel empirical approach. Frontiers in human neuroscience 2012;6:199.

REFERENCES

14 Hao X, Wang K, Li W, et al. Individual differences in brain structure and resting brain function underlie cognitive styles: evidence from the embedded figures test. PloS one 2013;8(12):e78089.

15 Oxford Dictionary of English–3rd Edition. 3rd edition ed. Oxford, UK: Oxford University Press, 2010.

16 De Pauw SS, Mervielde I, Van Leeuwen KG, De Clercq BJ. How temperament and personality contribute to the maladjustment of children with autism. Journal of autism and developmental disorders 2011 Feb;41(2):196-212.

17 Henriques G, (When) Are You Neurotic?, Theory of Knowledge: Psychology Today; 2012   23 Nov 2012, http://www.psychologytoday.com/blog/theory-knowledge/201211/when-are-you-neurotic

18 Ham BJ, Kim YH, Choi MJ, Cha JH, Choi YK, Lee MS. Serotonergic genes and personality traits in the Korean population. Neuroscience letters 2004 Jan 2;354(1):2-5.

19 Gonda X, Fountoulakis KN, Juhasz G, et al. Association of the s allele of the 5-HTTLPR with neuroticism-related traits and temperaments in a psychiatrically healthy population. Eur Arch Psychiatry Clin Neurosci 2009 Mar;259(2):106-13.

20 Chen C, Chen C, Moyzis R, et al. Contributions of dopamine-related genes and environmental factors to highly sensitive personality: a multi-step neuronal system-level approach. PloS one 2011;6(7):e21636.

21 Vinkhuyzen AA, Pedersen NL, Yang J, et al. Common SNPs explain some of the variation in the personality dimensions of neuroticism and extraversion. Translational psychiatry 2012;2:e102.

22 Caspi A, Hariri AR, Holmes A, Uher R, Moffitt TE. Genetic sensitivity to the environment: the case of the serotonin transporter gene and its implications for studying complex diseases and traits. The American journal of psychiatry 2010 May;167(5):509-27.

23 Felten A, Montag C, Markett S, Walter NT, Reuter M. Genetically determined dopamine availability predicts disposition for depression. Brain and behavior 2011 Nov;1(2):109-18.

24 Krueger RF, South S, Johnson W, Iacono W. The heritability of personality is not always 50%: gene-environment interactions and correlations between personality and parenting. Journal of personality 2008 Dec;76(6):1485-522.

25 Johnson W, Turkheimer E, Gottesman, II, Bouchard TJ, Jr. Beyond Heritability: Twin Studies in Behavioral Research. Current directions in psychological science 2010 Aug 1;18(4):217-20.

26 Spratt EG, Nicholas JS, Brady KT, et al. Enhanced cortisol response to stress in children in autism. Journal of autism and developmental disorders 2012 Jan;42(1):75-81.

27 Watkins A. Being brilliant every single day–Part 1. 2012   cited 2 March 2012; Available from: http://www.youtube.com/watch?v=q06YIWCR2Js

28 Dixon T. "Emotion": The History of a Keyword in Crisis. Emotion review : journal of the International Society for Research on Emotion 2012 Oct;4(4):338-44.

29 Elliott R. Executive functions and their disorders Imaging in clinical neuroscience. British medical bulletin 2003;65(1):49-59.

30 Marien H, Custers R, Hassin RR, Aarts H. Unconscious goal activation and the hijacking of the executive function. Journal of personality and social psychology 2012 Sep;103(3):399-415.

31 Wolff S. The history of autism. European child & adolescent psychiatry 2004 Aug;13(4):201-8.

32 WebMD: The history of autism. 2013 cited 2013 August 14; Available from: http://www.webmd.com/brain/autism/history-of-autism

33 Abrahams BS, Geschwind DH. Advances in autism genetics: on the threshold of a new neurobiology. Nature Reviews Genetics 2008;9(5):341-55.

34 Geschwind DH. Genetics of autism spectrum disorders. Trends in cognitive sciences 2011 Sep;15(9):409-16.

35 Won H, Mah W, Kim E. Autism spectrum disorder causes, mechanisms, and treatments: focus on neuronal synapses. Frontiers in molecular neuroscience 2013;6:19.

36 Chow ML, Pramparo T, Winn ME, et al. Age-dependent brain gene expression and copy number anomalies in autism suggest distinct pathological processes at young versus mature ages. PLoS genetics 2012;8(3):e1002592.

37 Schmidt RJ, Tancredi DJ, Ozonoff S, et al. Maternal periconceptional folic acid intake and risk of autism spectrum disorders and developmental delay in the CHARGE (CHildhood Autism Risks from Genetics and Environment) case-control study. The American journal of clinical nutrition 2012 Jul;96(1):80-9.

38 Mbadiwe T, Millis RM. Epigenetics and Autism. Autism research and treatment 2013;2013:826156.

39 Volk HE, Hertz-Picciotto I, Delwiche L, Lurmann F, McConnell R. Residential proximity to freeways and autism in the CHARGE study. Environmental health perspectives 2011 Jun;119(6):873-7.

40 Zerbo O, Iosif AM, Walker C, Ozonoff S, Hansen RL, Hertz-Picciotto I. Is maternal influenza or fever during pregnancy associated with autism or developmental delays? Results from the CHARGE (CHildhood Autism Risks from Genetics and Environment) study. Journal of autism and developmental disorders 2013 Jan;43(1):25-33.

41 Rai D, Lee BK, Dalman C, Golding J, Lewis G, Magnusson C. Parental depression, maternal antidepressant use during pregnancy, and risk of autism spectrum disorders: population based case-control study. Bmj 2013;346:f2059.

42 Christensen J, Gronborg TK, Sorensen MJ, et al. Prenatal valproate exposure and risk of autism spectrum disorders and childhood autism. JAMA : the journal of the American Medical Association 2013 Apr 24;309(16):1696-703.

REFERENCES

43 Suren P, Roth C, Bresnahan M, et al. Association between maternal use of folic acid supplements and risk of autism spectrum disorders in children. JAMA : the journal of the American Medical Association 2013 Feb 13;309(6):570-7.

44 Lyall K, Munger KL, O'Reilly EJ, Santangelo SL, Ascherio A. Maternal dietary fat intake in association with autism spectrum disorders. American journal of epidemiology 2013 Jul 15;178(2):209-20.

45 O'Roak BJ, Vives L, Girirajan S, et al. Sporadic autism exomes reveal a highly interconnected protein network of de novo mutations. Nature 2012 May 10;485(7397):246-50.

46 Courchesne E, Carper R, Akshoomoff N. Evidence of brain overgrowth in the first year of life in autism. JAMA : the journal of the American Medical Association 2003 Jul 16;290(3):337-44.

47 Shen MD, Nordahl CW, Young GS, et al. Early brain enlargement and elevated extra-axial fluid in infants who develop autism spectrum disorder. Brain : a journal of neurology 2013 Sep;136(Pt 9):2825-35.

48 Courchesne E, Mouton PR, Calhoun ME, et al. Neuron number and size in prefrontal cortex of children with autism. JAMA : the journal of the American Medical Association 2011 Nov 9;306(18):2001-10.

49 Eyler LT, Pierce K, Courchesne E. A failure of left temporal cortex to specialize for language is an early emerging and fundamental property of autism. Brain : a journal of neurology 2012 Mar;135(Pt 3):949-60.

50 Fatemi SH, Aldinger KA, Ashwood P, et al. Consensus paper: pathological role of the cerebellum in autism. Cerebellum 2012 Sep;11(3):777-807.

51 Onore C, Careaga M, Ashwood P. The role of immune dysfunction in the pathophysiology of autism. Brain Behav Immun 2012 Mar;26(3):383-92.

52 Moon C, Cooper RP, Fifer WP. Two-day-olds prefer their native language. Infant behavior and development 1993;16(4):495-500.

53 Pierce K. Exploring the Causes of Autism–The Role of Genetics and The Environment (Keynote Symposium 11). Asia Pacific Autism Conference; 2013 10 August; Adelaide, Australia: APAC 2013; 2013.

54 Pierce K, Müller RA, Ambrose J, Allen G, Courchesne E. Face processing occurs outside the fusiform `face area' in autism: evidence from functional MRI. Brain : a journal of neurology 2001 October 1, 2001;124(10):2059-73.

55 Bal E, Harden E, Lamb D, Van Hecke AV, Denver JW, Porges SW. Emotion recognition in children with autism spectrum disorders: relations to eye gaze and autonomic state. Journal of autism and developmental disorders 2010 Mar;40(3):358-70.

56 Harms MB, Martin A, Wallace GL. Facial emotion recognition in autism spectrum disorders: a review of behavioral and neuroimaging studies. Neuropsychology review 2010 Sep;20(3):290-322.

57 Nakamura K, Sekine Y, Ouchi Y, et al. Brain serotonin and dopamine transporter bindings in adults with high-functioning autism. Archives of general psychiatry 2010 Jan;67(1):59-68.

58 Austin EJ. Personality correlates of the broader autism phenotype as assessed by the Autism Spectrum Quotient (AQ). Personality and Individual Differences 2005;38(2):451-60.

59 Wakabayashi A, Baron-Cohen S, Wheelwright S. Are autistic traits an independent personality dimension? A study of the Autism-Spectrum Quotient (AQ) and the NEO-PI-R. Personality and Individual Differences 2006;41:873-83.

60 Schumann CM, Hamstra J, Goodlin-Jones BL, et al. The amygdala is enlarged in children but not adolescents with autism; the hippocampus is enlarged at all ages. The Journal of neuroscience : the official journal of the Society for Neuroscience 2004 Jul 14;24(28):6392-401.

61 Romero-Munguía MAn. Mnesic Imbalance and the Neuroanatomy of Autism Spectrum Disorders. In: Eapen V, editor. Autism—A Neurodevelopmental Journey from Genes to Behaviour. 1st ed: InTech, 2011;425-44.

62 De Sousa A. Towards an integrative theory of consciousness: part 1 (neurobiological and cognitive models). Mens sana monographs 2013 Jan;11(1):100-50.

63 Wing L. Asperger's syndrome: a clinical account. Psychological medicine 1981 Feb;11(1):115-29.

64 Quote Investigator, Everybody is a Genius. But If You Judge a Fish by Its Ability to Climb a Tree, It Will Live Its Whole Life Believing that It is Stupid., Quote Investigator—Exploring the origins of quotations; 2013 Apr 6, http://quoteinvestigator.com/2013/04/06/fish-climb/

65 Wu YL, Ding YP, Gao J, Tanaka Y, Zhang W. Risk factors and primary prevention trials for type 1 diabetes. International journal of biological sciences 2013;9(7):666-79.

66 Tuomilehto J, Lindstrom J, Eriksson JG, et al. Prevention of type 2 diabetes mellitus by changes in lifestyle among subjects with impaired glucose tolerance. The New England journal of medicine 2001 May 3;344(18):1343-50.

67 Beyond Entertainment / Discovery Channel. Battle of the sexes: Round 2 (Season 14, Episode 5). In: Beyond Entertainment / Discovery Channel, editor. Mythbusters: Discovery Channel, 2013;44min.

68 Harris R. Embracing Your Demons: an Overview of Acceptance and Commitment Therapy. Psychotherapy In Australia 2006;12(6):1-8.

69 Hayes SC, Luoma JB, Bond FW, Masuda A, Lillis J. Acceptance and Commitment Therapy: Model, processes and outcomes. Psychology Faculty Publications Paper 101. Department of Psychology: ScholarWorks @ Georgia State University, 2006.

70 Ost LG. Efficacy of the third wave of behavioral therapies: a systematic review and meta-analysis. Behaviour research and therapy 2008 Mar;46(3):296-321.

71 Powers MB, Zum Vorde Sive Vording MB, Emmelkamp PM. Acceptance and commitment therapy: a meta-analytic review. Psychotherapy and psychosomatics 2009;78(2):73-80.

72 Ruiz FJ. A review of Acceptance and Commitment Therapy (ACT) empirical evidence: Correlational, experimental psychopathology, component and outcome studies. International Journal of Psychology and Psychological Therapy 2010;10(1):125-62.

73 Ruiz FJ. Acceptance and Commitment Therapy versus Traditional Cognitive Behavioral Therapy: A Systematic Review and Meta-analysis of Current Empirical Evidence. International journal of psychology and psychological therapy 2012;12(3):333-58.

74 Harris R. The happiness trap : how to stop struggling and start living. Boston: Trumpeter, 2008.

75 Lozada M, D'Adamo P, Fuentes MA. Beneficial effects of human altruism. Journal of theoretical biology 2011 Nov 21;289:12-6.

76 Keng SL, Smoski MJ, Robins CJ. Effects of mindfulness on psychological health: a review of empirical studies. Clinical psychology review 2011 Aug;31(6):1041-56.

77 Barry VW, Baruth M, Beets MW, Durstine JL, Liu J, Blair SN. Fitness vs. fatness on all-cause mortality: a meta-analysis. Progress in cardiovascular diseases 2014 Jan-Feb;56(4):382-90.

78 Lavie CJ, McAuley PA, Church TS, Milani RV, Blair SN. Obesity and cardiovascular diseases: implications regarding fitness, fatness, and severity in the obesity paradox. Journal of the American College of Cardiology 2014 Apr 15;63(14):1345-54.

79 Moylan S, Eyre HA, Maes M, Baune BT, Jacka FN, Berk M. Exercising the worry away: how inflammation, oxidative and nitrogen stress mediates the beneficial effect of physical activity on anxiety disorder symptoms and behaviours. Neuroscience and biobehavioral reviews 2013 May;37(4):573-84.

80 Wood AM, Froh JJ, Geraghty AW. Gratitude and well-being: a review and theoretical integration. Clinical psychology review 2010 Nov;30(7):890-905.

81 Worthington EL, Jr., Witvliet CV, Pietrini P, Miller AJ. Forgiveness, health, and well-being: a review of evidence for emotional versus decisional forgiveness, dispositional forgivingness, and reduced unforgiveness. Journal of behavioral medicine 2007 Aug;30(4):291-302.

82 Lawler KA, Younger JW, Piferi RL, Jobe RL, Edmondson KA, Jones WH. The unique effects of forgiveness on health: an exploration of pathways. Journal of behavioral medicine 2005 Apr;28(2):157-67.

83 Strang S, Utikal V, Fischbacher U, Weber B, Falk A. Neural correlates of receiving an apology and active forgiveness: an FMRI study. PloS one 2014;9(2):e87654.

84 Brent LJ, Chang SW, Gariepy JF, Platt ML. The neuroethology of friendship. Annals of the New York Academy of Sciences 2014 May;1316:1-17.

85 Holt-Lunstad J, Smith TB, Layton JB. Social relationships and mortality risk: a meta-analytic review. PLoS medicine 2010 Jul;7(7):e1000316.

86 Luo Y, Hawkley LC, Waite LJ, Cacioppo JT. Loneliness, health, and mortality in old age: a national longitudinal study. Social science & medicine 2012 Mar;74(6):907-14.

87 Oh HJ, Ozkaya E, LaRose R. How does online social networking enhance life satisfaction? The relationships among online supportive interaction, affect, perceived social support, sense of community, and life satisfaction. Computers in Human Behavior 2014;30:69-78.

88 What Is Stress. cited 2013 July; Available from: http://www.stress.org/what-is-stress/

89 Shweder RA. America's Latest Export: A Stressed-Out World. The New York Times. 1997 26 January 1997.

90 McEwen BS. Protective and damaging effects of stress mediators: central role of the brain. Dialogues in clinical neuroscience 2006;8(4):367-81.

91 Hackney AC. Stress and the neuroendocrine system: the role of exercise as a stressor and modifier of stress. Expert review of endocrinology & metabolism 2006 Nov 1;1(6):783-92.

92 Beyond Entertainment / Discovery Channel. The Alaska Special 2 (Season 7, Episode 2). Mythbusters: Discovery Channel, 2009;44min.

93 Gravity Hurts (So Good). NASA Science | Science News 2001 cited July 2013; Available from: http://science1.nasa.gov/science-news/science-at-nasa/2001/ast02aug_1/

94 van Loon JJ. Hypergravity studies in the Netherlands. Journal of gravitational physiology : a journal of the International Society for Gravitational Physiology 2001 Jul;8(1):P139-42.

95 McHugh J. Surviving 7G. Wired. 2003.

96 Hortobagyi T, Maffiuletti NA. Neural adaptations to electrical stimulation strength training. European journal of applied physiology 2011 Oct;111(10):2439-49.

97 Schoenfeld BJ. The mechanisms of muscle hypertrophy and their application to resistance training. Journal of strength and conditioning research / National Strength & Conditioning Association 2010 Oct;24(10):2857-72.

98 Adversity. Demotivators cited July 2013; Available from: http://www.despair.com/adversity.html

99 Petrik D, Lagace DC, Eisch AJ. The neurogenesis hypothesis of affective and anxiety disorders: are we mistaking the scaffolding for the building? Neuropharmacology 2012 Jan;62(1):21-34.

100 Wu G, Feder A, Cohen H, et al. Understanding resilience. Frontiers in behavioral neuroscience 2013;7:10.

101 Skinner EA, Zimmer-Gembeck MJ. The development of coping. Annual review of psychology 2007;58:119-44.

102 Connor-Smith JK, Flachsbart C. Relations between personality and coping: a meta-analysis. Journal of personality and social psychology 2007;93(6):1080.

103 Penley JA, Tomaka J. Associations among the Big Five, emotional responses, and coping with acute stress. Personality and individual differences 2002;32(7):1215-28.

104 Bouchard G. Cognitive appraisals, neuroticism, and openness as correlates of coping strategies: An integrative model of adptation to marital difficulties. Canadian Journal of Behavioural Science/Revue canadienne des sciences du comportement 2003;35(1):1.

105 Forgas JP, East R. On being happy and gullible: Mood effects on skepticism and the detection of deception. Journal of Experimental Social Psychology 2008;44:1362-7.

106 Kato K, Pedersen NL. Personality and coping: A study of twins reared apart and twins reared together. Behavior genetics 2005;35(2):147-58.

107 Dreher J-C, Kohn P, Kolachana B, Weinberger DR, Berman KF. Variation in dopamine genes influences responsivity of the human reward system. Proceedings of the National Academy of Sciences 2009;106(2):617-22.

108 Ullsperger M. Genetic association studies of performance monitoring and learning from feedback: the role of dopamine and serotonin. Neuroscience & Biobehavioral Reviews 2010;34(5):649-59.

109 Russo SJ, Murrough JW, Han M-H, Charney DS, Nestler EJ. Neurobiology of resilience. Nature neuroscience 2012 November;15(11):1475-84.

110 Verma R, Balhara YP, Gupta CS. Gender differences in stress response: Role of developmental and biological determinants. Industrial psychiatry journal 2011 Jan;20(1):4-10.

111 McEwen BS, Wingfield JC. What is in a name? Integrating homeostasis, allostasis and stress. Hormones and behavior 2010 Feb;57(2):105-11.

112 Chrousos GP. Stress and disorders of the stress system. Nature reviews Endocrinology 2009 Jul;5(7):374-81.

113 McEwen BS. Stressed or stressed out: what is the difference? Journal of psychiatry & neuroscience : JPN 2005 Sep;30(5):315-8.

114 Lee BH, Kim YK. The roles of BDNF in the pathophysiology of major depression and in antidepressant treatment. Psychiatry Investig 2010 Dec;7(4):231-5.

115 Jallo N, Bourguignon C, Taylor AG, Ruiz J, Goehler L. The biobehavioral effects of relaxation guided imagery on maternal stress. Advances in mind-body medicine 2009 Winter;24(4):12-22.

116 Trakhtenberg EC. The effects of guided imagery on the immune system: a critical review. The International journal of neuroscience 2008 Jun;118(6):839-55.

117 Baird CL, Sands L. A pilot study of the effectiveness of guided imagery with progressive muscle relaxation to reduce chronic pain and mobility difficulties of osteoarthritis. Pain management nursing : official journal of the American Society of Pain Management Nurses 2004 Sep;5(3):97-104.

118 Morone NE, Greco CM. Mind-body interventions for chronic pain in older adults: a structured review. Pain medicine 2007 May-Jun;8(4):359-75.

119 Fletcher GF, Balady G, Blair SN, et al. Statement on exercise: benefits and recommendations for physical activity programs for all Americans. A statement for health professionals by the Committee on Exercise and Cardiac Rehabilitation of the Council on Clinical Cardiology, American Heart Association. Circulation 1996 Aug 15;94(4):857-62.

120 Warburton DE, Nicol CW, Bredin SS. Health benefits of physical activity: the evidence. CMAJ : Canadian Medical Association journal = journal de l'Association medicale canadienne 2006 Mar 14;174(6):801-9.

121 Rimer J, Dwan K, Lawlor DA, et al. Exercise for depression. The Cochrane database of systematic reviews 2012;7:CD004366.

122 DeBoer LB, Powers MB, Utschig AC, Otto MW, Smits JA. Exploring exercise as an avenue for the treatment of anxiety disorders. Expert review of neurotherapeutics 2012 Aug;12(8):1011-22.

123 MacDonald RA. Music, health, and well-being: a review. International journal of qualitative studies on health and well-being 2013;8:20635.

124 Knox D, Beveridge S, Mitchell LA, MacDonald RA. Acoustic analysis and mood classification of pain-relieving music. The Journal of the Acoustical Society of America 2011 Sep;130(3):1673-82.

125 Field T, Diego M, Hernandez-Reif M. Preterm infant massage therapy research: a review. Infant behavior & development 2010 Apr;33(2):115-24.

126 Moraska A, Pollini RA, Boulanger K, Brooks MZ, Teitlebaum L. Physiological adjustments to stress measures following massage therapy: a review of the literature. Evidence-based complementary and alternative medicine : eCAM 2010 Dec;7(4):409-18.

127 Bested AC, Logan AC, Selhub EM. Intestinal microbiota, probiotics and mental health: from Metchnikoff to modern advances: Part II–contemporary contextual research. Gut pathogens 2013;5(1):3.

128 Bested AC, Logan AC, Selhub EM. Intestinal microbiota, probiotics and mental health: from Metchnikoff to modern advances: part III–convergence toward clinical trials. Gut pathogens 2013;5(1):4.

129 Gump BB, Matthews KA. Are vacations good for your health? The 9-year mortality experience after the multiple risk factor intervention trial. Psychosomatic medicine 2000 Sep-Oct;62(5):608-12.

130 Liu RT, Alloy LB. Stress generation in depression: A systematic review of the empirical literature and recommendations for future study. Clinical psychology review 2010 Jul;30(5):582-93.

131 Duman RS, Li N. A neurotrophic hypothesis of depression: role of synaptogenesis in the actions of NMDA receptor antagonists. Philosophical transactions of the Royal Society of London Series B, Biological sciences 2012 Sep 5;367(1601):2475-84.

132 Hauger RL, Risbrough V, Oakley RH, Olivares-Reyes JA, Dautzenberg FM. Role of CRF receptor signaling in stress vulnerability, anxiety, and depression. Annals of the New York Academy of Sciences 2009 Oct;1179:120-43.

133 Shear MK. Grief and mourning gone awry: pathway and course of complicated grief. Dialogues in clinical neuroscience 2012 Jun;14(2):119-28.

134 Karatsoreos IN, McEwen BS. Resilience and vulnerability: a neurobiological perspective. F1000prime reports 2013;5:13.

135 Hansell NK, Wright MJ, Medland SE, et al. Genetic co-morbidity between neuroticism, anxiety/depression and somatic distress in a population sample of adolescent and young adult twins. Psychological medicine 2012 Jun;42(6):1249-60.

136 Boardman JD, Alexander KB, Stallings MC. Stressful life events and depression among adolescent twin pairs. Biodemography and social biology 2011;57(1):53-66.

137 Anderson I. Depression. The Treatment and Management of Depression in Adults (Update). NICE clinical guideline 90.2009. London: The British Psychological Society and The Royal College of Psychiatrists, 2010.

138 Lai JS, Hiles S, Bisquera A, Hure AJ, McEvoy M, Attia J. A systematic review and meta-analysis of dietary patterns and depression in community-dwelling adults. The American journal of clinical nutrition 2014 Jan;99(1):181-97.

139 NowOK. Cognitive Behavioural Therapy. Dictionary of Psychotherapy 2015 cited; Available from: http://www.dictionary.nowok.co.uk/cognitive-behavioural-therapy-cbt.php

140 Longmore RJ, Worrell M. Do we need to challenge thoughts in cognitive behavior therapy? Clinical psychology review 2007 Mar;27(2):173-87.

141 Dobson KS, Hollon SD, Dimidjian S, et al. Randomized trial of behavioral activation, cognitive therapy, and antidepressant medication in the prevention of relapse and recurrence in major depression. Journal of consulting and clinical psychology 2008 Jun;76(3):468-77.

142 Smout M. Acceptance and commitment therapy—pathways for general practitioners. Aust Fam Physician 2012 Sep;41(9):672-6.

143 Wurm C, Robertson M, Rushton P. Interpersonal psychotherapy: An overview. Psychotherapy in Australia 2008;14(3):46.

144 Boelens PA, Reeves RR, Replogle WH, Koenig HG. A randomized trial of the effect of prayer on depression and anxiety. Int J Psychiatry Med 2009;39(4):377-92.

145 Grupe DW, Nitschke JB. Uncertainty and anticipation in anxiety: an integrated neurobiological and psychological perspective. Nature reviews Neuroscience 2013 Jul;14(7):488-501.

146 Duman EA, Canli T. Influence of life stress, 5-HTTLPR genotype, and SLC6A4 methylation on gene expression and stress response in healthy Caucasian males. Biol Mood Anxiety Disord 2015;5:2.

147 Porges SW. The polyvagal perspective. Biological psychology 2007 Feb;74(2):116-43.

148 James AC, James G, Cowdrey FA, Soler A, Choke A. Cognitive behavioural therapy for anxiety disorders in children and adolescents. The Cochrane database of systematic reviews 2013;6:CD004690.

149 Swain J, Hancock K, Hainsworth C, Bowman J. Acceptance and commitment therapy in the treatment of anxiety: a systematic review. Clinical psychology review 2013 Dec;33(8):965-78.

150 Quide Y, Witteveen AB, El-Hage W, Veltman DJ, Olff M. Differences between effects of psychological versus pharmacological treatments on functional and morphological brain alterations in anxiety disorders and major depressive disorder: a systematic review. Neuroscience and biobehavioral reviews 2012 Jan;36(1):626-44.

151 Sokolowski K, Corbin JG. Wired for behaviors: from development to function of innate limbic system circuitry. Frontiers in molecular neuroscience 2012;5:55.

152 Howes OD, Fusar-Poli P, Bloomfield M, Selvaraj S, McGuire P. From the prodrome to chronic schizophrenia: the neurobiology underlying psychotic symptoms and cognitive impairments. Curr Pharm Des 2012;18(4):459-65.

153 Der-Avakian A, Markou A. The neurobiology of anhedonia and other reward-related deficits. Trends Neurosci 2012 Jan;35(1):68-77.

154 Gold JM, Strauss GP, Waltz JA, Robinson BM, Brown JK, Frank MJ. Negative symptoms of schizophrenia are associated with abnormal effort-cost computations. Biological psychiatry 2013 Jul 15;74(2):130-6.

155 Williams GV, Castner SA. Under the curve: critical issues for elucidating D1 receptor function in working memory. Neuroscience 2006 Apr 28;139(1):263-76.

156 Greenwood TA, Lazzeroni LC, Murray SS, et al. Analysis of 94 candidate genes and 12 endophenotypes for schizophrenia from the Consortium on the Genetics of Schizophrenia. The American journal of psychiatry 2011 Sep;168(9):930-46.

157 Howes OD, Murray RM. Schizophrenia: an integrated sociodevelopmental-cognitive model. Lancet 2014 May 10;383(9929):1677-87.

158 Khandaker GM, Cousins L, Deakin J, Lennox BR, Yolken R, Jones PB. Inflammation and immunity in schizophrenia: implications for pathophysiology and treatment. Lancet Psychiatry 2015 Mar;2(3):258-70.

159 Melnik T, Soares BG, Puga MEdS, Atallah ÁN. Efficacy and safety of atypical antipsychotic drugs (quetiapine, risperidone, aripiprazole and paliperidone) compared with placebo or typical antipsychotic drugs for treating refractory schizophrenia: overview of systematic reviews. Sao Paulo Medical Journal 2010;128:141-66.

160 Leucht S, Tardy M, Komossa K, et al. Antipsychotic drugs versus placebo for relapse prevention in schizophrenia: a systematic review and meta-analysis. Lancet 2012 Jun 2;379(9831):2063-71.

161 Torniainen M, Mittendorfer-Rutz E, Tanskanen A, et al. Antipsychotic treatment and mortality in schizophrenia. Schizophrenia bulletin 2015 May;41(3):656-63.

162 Reutfors J, Bahmanyar S, Jonsson EG, et al. Medication and suicide risk in schizophrenia: a nested case-control study. Schizophrenia research 2013 Nov;150(2-3):416-20.

163 Jones C, Hacker D, Cormac I, Meaden A, Irving CB. Cognitive behaviour therapy versus other psychosocial treatments for schizophrenia. The Cochrane database of systematic reviews 2012;4:CD008712.

164 Lynch D, Laws KR, McKenna PJ. Cognitive behavioural therapy for major psychiatric disorder: does it really work? A meta-analytical review of well-controlled trials. Psychological medicine 2010 Jan;40(1):9-24.

165 Carson V, Huss K. Prayer--an effective therapeutic and teaching tool. J Psychiatr Nurs Ment Health Serv 1979 Mar;17(3):34-7.

166 Martin J, O'Donovan MC, Thapar A, Langley K, Williams N. The relative contribution of common and rare genetic variants to ADHD. Translational psychiatry 2015;5:e506.

167 Faraone SV, Perlis RH, Doyle AE, et al. Molecular genetics of attention-deficit/hyperactivity disorder. Biological psychiatry 2005 Jun 1;57(11):1313-23.

168 Akutagava-Martins GC, Salatino-Oliveira A, Kieling CC, Rohde LA, Hutz MH. Genetics of attention-deficit/hyperactivity disorder: current findings and future directions. Expert review of neurotherapeutics 2013 Apr;13(4):435-45.

169 Faraone SV, Mick E. Molecular genetics of attention deficit hyperactivity disorder. Psychiatr Clin North Am 2010 Mar;33(1):159-80.

170 Franke B, Neale BM, Faraone SV. Genome-wide association studies in ADHD. Hum Genet 2009 Jul;126(1):13-50.

171 Thapar A, Cooper M, Eyre O, Langley K. What have we learnt about the causes of ADHD? Journal of child psychology and psychiatry, and allied disciplines 2013 Jan;54(1):3-16.

172 Cherkasova M, Sulla EM, Dalena KL, Ponde MP, Hechtman L. Developmental course of attention deficit hyperactivity disorder and its predictors. J Can Acad Child Adolesc Psychiatry 2013 Feb;22(1):47-54.

173 Banaschewski T, Becker K, Scherag S, Franke B, Coghill D. Molecular genetics of attention-deficit/hyperactivity disorder: an overview. European child & adolescent psychiatry 2010 Mar;19(3):237-57.

174 Reichow B, Volkmar FR, Bloch MH. Systematic review and meta-analysis of pharmacological treatment of the symptoms of attention-deficit/hyperactivity disorder in children with pervasive developmental disorders. Journal of autism and developmental disorders 2013 Oct;43(10):2435-41.

175 Shaw P, Lerch J, Greenstein D, et al. Longitudinal mapping of cortical thickness and clinical outcome in children and adolescents with attention-deficit/hyperactivity disorder. Archives of general psychiatry 2006 May;63(5):540-9.

176 Cortese S. The neurobiology and genetics of Attention-Deficit/Hyperactivity Disorder (ADHD): what every clinician should know. European journal of paediatric neurology : EJPN : official journal of the European Paediatric Neurology Society 2012 Sep;16(5):422-33.

177 Cao M, Shu N, Cao Q, Wang Y, He Y. Imaging functional and structural brain connectomics in attention-deficit/hyperactivity disorder. Mol Neurobiol 2014 Dec;50(3):1111-23.

178 Strohl MP. Bradley's Benzedrine studies on children with behavioral disorders. Yale J Biol Med 2011 Mar;84(1):27-33.

179 Vysniauske R, Verburgh L, Oosterlaan J, Molendijk ML. The Effects of Physical Exercise on Functional Outcomes in the Treatment of ADHD: A Meta-Analysis. J Atten Disord 2016 Feb 9.

180 Sonuga-Barke EJ, Brandeis D, Cortese S, et al. Nonpharmacological interventions for ADHD: systematic review and meta-analyses of randomized controlled trials of dietary and psychological treatments. The American journal of psychiatry 2013 Mar 1;170(3):275-89.

181 Storebo OJ, Ramstad E, Krogh HB, et al. Methylphenidate for children and adolescents with attention deficit hyperactivity disorder (ADHD). The Cochrane database of systematic reviews 2015 Nov 25;11:CD009885.

182 Kanner L. Autistic disturbances of affective contact. Acta paedopsychiatrica 1968;35(4):100-36.

183 Baron-Cohen S. Leo Kanner, Hans Asperger, and the discovery of autism (Book review). Lancet 2015 Oct 3;386:1329-30.

184 Draaisma D. Stereotypes of autism. Philosophical transactions of the Royal Society of London Series B, Biological sciences 2009 May 27;364(1522):1475-80.

185 Baio J. Prevalence of Autism Spectrum Disorders: Autism and Developmental Disabilities Monitoring Network, 14 Sites, United States, 2008. Morbidity and Mortality Weekly Report. Surveillance Summaries. Volume 61, Number 3. Centers for Disease Control and Prevention 2012.

REFERENCES

186 Kim YS, Leventhal BL, Koh Y-J, et al. Prevalence of autism spectrum disorders in a total population sample. American Journal of Psychiatry 2011;168(9):904-12.

187 Cappelletti M, Lee HL, Freeman ED, Price CJ. The role of right and left parietal lobes in the conceptual processing of numbers. Journal of cognitive neuroscience 2010 Feb;22(2):331-46.

188 Demicheli V, Rivetti A, Debalini MG, Di Pietrantonj C. Vaccines for measles, mumps and rubella in children. The Cochrane database of systematic reviews 2012;2:CD004407.

189 Volkmar FR, Reichow B. Autism in DSM-5: progress and challenges. Molecular autism 2013;4(1):13.

190 Corso PS, Mercy JA, Simon TR, Finkelstein EA, Miller TR. Medical costs and productivity losses due to interpersonal and self-directed violence in the United States. Am J Prev Med 2007 Jun;32(6):474-82.

191 Cvinar JG. Do suicide survivors suffer social stigma: a review of the literature. Perspect Psychiatr Care 2005 Jan-Mar;41(1):14-21.

192 Knox KL, Litts DA, Talcott GW, Feig JC, Caine ED. Risk of suicide and related adverse outcomes after exposure to a suicide prevention programme in the US Air Force: cohort study. Bmj 2003 Dec 13;327(7428):1376.

193 Correll CU, Detraux J, De Lepeleire J, De Hert M. Effects of antipsychotics, antidepressants and mood stabilizers on risk for physical diseases in people with schizophrenia, depression and bipolar disorder. World psychiatry : official journal of the World Psychiatric Association 2015 Jun;14(2):119-36.

194 McDowell AK, Lineberry TW, Bostwick JM. Practical suicide-risk management for the busy primary care physician. Mayo Clinic proceedings 2011 Aug;86(8):792-800.

195 Wahl OF. Stigma as a barrier to recovery from mental illness. Trends in cognitive sciences 2012 Jan;16(1):9-10.

Acknowledgements

It's my turn to say #ThankYou to all the people who have made this book possible.

In 2 Corinthians 12:9, God said to Paul, "My grace is sufficient for you, for my power is made perfect in weakness." In my mental health journey, I have come to realise just that. I am weak, God is strong. God has put me back together (several times now), and it's His grace that binds my brokenness together and keeps me whole. For that, I'm forever thankful.

To my wife Sharon, for being the only person in the world who truly knows me—and is still married to me anyway. She has helped me through the darkest times in my life, and she continues to enable me to do the hard yards of research and writing so I can help others through the darkest times in their lives.

To my boys, Lachlan and Alex: my inspiration, my motivation, my frustration, my acclamation, and my adoration. I pray the Christian church that you will lead one day accepts and supports mental illness and its recovery in a way that shows the power of God's love like no other generation has seen.

Special thanks go to Melanie Page, Joelle Morgan and Dr Amy Weber for their insightful suggestions and constructive feedback on the manuscript. I also want to thank Rebekah Robinson from Beckon Creative for her assistance producing the Tap Model illustrations. Thank you to Matt and Nicole Danswan and the team at Ark House Publishing for bringing life into the manuscript and turning it into a tangible reality.

A very special thank you goes to Dr Jennifer Kahle, cognitive neuroscientist, for applying her wealth of neuroscientific knowledge, academic experience and her keen editorial eye to the manuscript. She truly went above and beyond. Her spirit of excellence has lifted the manuscript to a much higher level of polish and professionalism.

Finally, to every patient that I have seen over the last twenty years— I've learnt more from you than I ever did from all of the boring lectures and tutorials I ever went to. Little by little, day by day, you have taught me the science of health, the art of medicine, and the value of life.

About The Author

D r C. Edward Pitt MBBS FRACGP is a full time GP* and spare-time writer. He lives and works in the northern suburbs of Brisbane, Queensland, Australia.

He has been studying and working in the medical profession since 1992. He spent a number of years in hospital paediatrics before getting sick of shift-work and moving into general practice.

Since attaining his GP Fellowship in 2005, he has gained experience in many and varied areas of medicine including Skin Cancer Medicine, Cosmetic Medicine, Aged Care, and Sexual Health & Family Planning. He acts as an independent medico-legal expert in the field of general practice, and serves in executive positions on a number of national and state level boards for the Royal Australian College of General Practitioners.

His written work has been broadly published in a number of different spheres. In the early 2000's, he was a regular writer for the national Christian magazine, "Alive". He published his first book in 2009, "Stress Out", now in its second edition. In 2013, he published "Hold That Thought: Reappraising The Work of Dr Caroline Leaf", and in 2015, he published "Fats and Figures", a short book on heart health. In early 2016 his article, "Cutting through the Paleo hype: The evidence for the Palaeolithic diet" was published by the peer reviewed medical journal *Australian Family Physician*.

He is a husband, father to two rambunctious boys, coffee connoisseur, amateur actor and a terrible dancer.

Whatever time he has left, he usually wastes it on Facebook or Angry Birds!

(* GP is short for General Practitioner, also known as a Family Physician in some parts of the world)

CPSIA information can be obtained
at www.ICGtesting.com
Printed in the USA
LVOW03s1231140817
544948LV00019B/851/P